D1569145

The Many Americas
Shall Be One

Books by Harrison E. Salisbury

THE MANY AMERICAS SHALL BE ONE

WAR BETWEEN RUSSIA AND CHINA

THE 900 DAYS: *The Siege of Leningrad*

ORBIT OF CHINA

BEHIND THE LINES–HANOI

THE NORTHERN PALMYRA AFFAIR

A NEW RUSSIA?

MOSCOW JOURNAL–THE END OF STALIN

TO MOSCOW AND BEYOND

THE SHOOK-UP GENERATION

AMERICAN IN RUSSIA

RUSSIA ON THE WAY

HARRISON E. SALISBURY

The Many Americas Shall Be One

W · W · NORTON & COMPANY · INC · New York

Copyright © 1971 by Harrison E. Salisbury

FIRST EDITION

SBN   393 05437 3
Library of Congress Catalog Card No. 70-144093

ALL RIGHTS RESERVED

Published simultaneously in Canada
by George J. McLeod Limited, Toronto

PRINTED IN THE UNITED STATES OF AMERICA

1   2   3   4   5   6   7   8   9   0

For Charlotte and John, Sue and Michael,
Rosina and Scott, Gretchen and Stephan,
Ellen and Curtis, and all the others who
will make the many Americas one.

Contents

Author's Note

This book is written in hope, not despair, in confidence, not doubt. The title is a gloss on Che Guevara's famous declaration of April 16, 1967—"How close and bright would the future appear if two, three, many Vietnams, flowered on the face of the globe." America's future is bright for a different reason—not because of the "quota of death and immense tragedies," the "daily heroism," the "repeated blows against imperialism" of which Guevara spoke, but because "two, three, many Americas" exist, contend, challenge, and from which, I believe, will emerge a new and whole America, robust, bright, noble, equitable, gifted with grace, a certain wisdom, and self-knowledge.

The Many Americas
Shall Be One

CHAPTER 1

A Day in May

I am writing this on a cool, gray day in May. The field outside my window sparkles with the gold of dandelions and the dust yellow of mustard. A fox sparrow chirps in the grass and a cowbird, black as squid, preens on the stone wall.

That is the way it looks from my window. But I am composing no nature story, no countryman's vignette, no counterpoint to the thunder of the bombs as they carpet Cambodian jungles with napalm, black and red, no rural escape hatch from the shout of the hard hats, the stench of the tear gas, the smell of blood and vomit on the campus green, the mold of the garbage, the sick sweet breath of heroin, the riot guns, the obscenities, the sour taste of fear and futility that creeps across the land.

The times are bad. The question—the *only* question—is how bad? Can we turn them around, forge good from evil, fashion a decent today and a bright tomorrow from within the jaws of disaster?

I have no ready answer for that question. Any man who offers one is a fool or a charlatan, for we have entered a new valley in time in which there is not one institution or symbol, not one principle or conviction, not one convention or style, no way of life, no hallowed belief, no hoary tradition, no seat of authority not under challenge.

While it may sometimes seem to us that we inhabit the very heart of a maelstrom, there are those in far places—in the Vatican, in the crowded universities of Japan, in secret rendezvous of ancient Arab cities, within the Kremlin, or the squares of Peking—who feel that they, not we, stand at the epicenter of world cataclysm.

No doubt we are ethnocentric in our response to the shaking of the world. We see it as the shaking of *our* world. The silent spring of Rachel Carson was *our* silent spring, *our* robins vanished. The race question is *our* question, the specifics of blacks and whites in America, not the clash of Ibo and Yoruba in Nigeria. Genocide in *our* lexicon refers to U.S. policy in Southeast Asia, not to the Brazilian predators who use toxins and Sten guns to wipe out inconvenient primitives along the upper Amazon.

No need to labor the point. Symptoms of revolutionary change, systemic crisis, decay of social tradition may be more acute in the United States than elsewhere; or this may simply be our own perception—the way it seems to us.

Certain it is that we are surrounded by evidences that the Old Order Changeth—mixed nude bathing in the Washington reflecting pool; nuns in short skirts and priests gone underground with revolutionary aims; copulation in every Krafft-Ebing variation on drive-in movie screens; black and white students shot down by troops wearing "USA" on their shoulderpatches; black revolutionaries exterminated with the brutality of South Africa's Sharpville; dedicated dynamiters blowing themselves, other young people, university and federal buildings into a shambles; the pill and Blue Cross abortion instead of Hester Prynne; Naderism, or social responsibility, not profits, as the touchstone of corporation management; anticulture (junk furs, found objects, Campbell Soup cans, camp, walk-on painting, walk-in sculpture); and, of course, the challenge direct to the whole American Establishment.

What has been left out of that compendium? Very little. And any omission is accidental. Because the challenge is total. Not that one person, one critic, one movement comprehends the whole. None does. But somewhere someone has zeroed in on every target contained in a catalogue of the American way; the aim is fixed; the guns are going. No need to ask for whom the bullet in the Cleveland ghetto was intended; the victim is you, and me, our children, black, yellow or white—the victim is America (and so, God save us, is the assassin).

Eminent historians solemnly affirm that the American crisis is more deep than any since 1933 (Arthur Schlesinger, Jr.) or 1861 (Richard Hofstadter). But what does this mean? True, in 1933 American society was pulled apart by economic catastrophe. The collapse of a pink-and-silver Hollywood vision of Prosperity Unlimited turned us back upon ourselves, challenging, reexamining (or so we thought) every premise of the system which had destroyed our dream. We anathematized poor Herbert Hoover, perhaps the least blameworthy of leaders. It was Calvin Coolidge's granite philosophy—"they hired the money, didn't they?"—and Warren G. Harding's graft which paved the way to 1929, not Mr. Hoover's Quakerism. We ranged randomly over the field of political pick-me-ups. Some turned to communism, little knowing that Stalin long since had poisoned its dream. Some to populism and free silver (Huey P. Long, Father Coughlin). Some to pseudo-socio-science (the Technocrats, Dr. Townsend). Some escaped to the hills of Vermont or the wilderness of Montana. Some ran off to Paris. Some shot themselves. The most profound emotion was despair, disillusion, despondency, the bitterness of the child whose candy is snatched from his hands, who gets no birthday cake, whose carousel becomes a treadmill. In those years the American dream turned brown at the edges, curled up, fell from the money tree, and was whisked away never to return by chill and vagrant winds. *Never to return?*

Oh, yes. Never to return. That was the way it seemed. I remember those days. Each is etched in acid in my memory.

One afternoon in February, 1933, I got on the New York Central's Detroit Flyer in Chicago, carrying an alligator gladstone bag which I kept beside me in the day-coach seat. The bank holiday had been declared in Detroit and in the alligator bag I had $300 in nickels, dimes, quarters, half-dollars (half-dollars still circulated in those days). I was a young reporter for United Press and the money was to enable our Detroit bureau to function—money for phone calls, taxicabs, buses, cigarettes, lunch-counter tabs, needle beer, all the things you had to have money for. The banks in Chicago were still open. They did not close until a few days later along with all the other banks in the country.

I slumped in my coach seat, my eyes glued to the window, one foot constantly touching the alligator bag lest it get away from me. I had never had $300 in my possession before. As the train neared Detroit it roared through the great industrial suburbs. We passed the Chrysler works. Not a wisp of smoke from the high stacks. We passed the great G.M. works. Closed tight. Only at one point did I see a thin plume of white steam rising in the late afternoon sunlight—a steam boiler, probably, providing heat to keep machinery from damage. The gates were high, meshed wire, shut and locked. The same was true of Ford's. Not a chimney with smoke issuing from it. Detroit was dead. Along the Detroit River sprawled thousands upon thousands of lean-tos and shacks, tin-can towns, caves hollowed in the raggedy clay sides. Only there was smoke to be seen—smoke from hundreds of campfires, hundreds of tin-can kettles and mulligan stew, the glow of the fires along the river like a hundred ruby eyes in the dusk, silhouetting the dark hulks of the great factories—the world's greatest industrial complex, the heart and pride of America, the special and spectacular U.S.

contribution to technology—the assembly-line production system, the high wage system (Henry Ford's famous $5 a day for ordinary workers in World War I)—dead, finished, slaughtered, done-away-with-from-within. I was young and excited. I kept a notebook on my knees jotting down impressions. Never in my lifetime, I thought, will they get it going again. Never again will the smoke pour from the stacks of River Rouge. The whole thing is broken and no one can put the pieces together. The American system has ended. I did not know what could come in its place. But I did know as surely as I was riding the Detroit Flyer, as surely as that alligator bag pressed my knees, that I was watching history unroll—the end of the American era.

The next morning I sat in the office of Frank Murphy, the radical young mayor of Detroit. It was divided by mahogany railings like a big bank lobby. Murphy sat at a desk within the railings, but out in the open where everyone could see and watch. As I waited my turn four or five men arrived—fine-looking, distinguished men, you knew they were civic leaders, important men, the moment you saw their trim black homburgs, the thin, fashionable mink lapels of their black broadcloth winter coats, the impeccable shine of their shoes. And one, I believe, carried a gold-headed stick. They came into the enclosure where Murphy, lithe, young, gaunt-faced, self-confident, rose to meet them and they stood there talking, still standing, just far enough away so that I could not hear every word but close enough so that I knew what they were talking about. They were the bankers of Detroit, the men who had had their hands at the throttle of the vast industrial machine. They were powerful men. Now, they held their hats in their hands. They stood up close to Murphy and they begged for help. Tears ran down the face of one man, his lips quivered as he talked, and Murphy, warm-hearted, embarrassed, a little shy, impulsively put one arm around him—the Irish, radical politician, trying in a human way to ease the pain. There was nothing more he could do. I don't

know what they wanted—some help, some aid, some reassurance
that was beyond the ability of Murphy or any man. What they
really wanted was what the youngster wanted when he appealed
to Shoeless Joe Jackson of the White Sox in 1919: "Say it ain't
so, Joe, say it ain't so."

But it *was* so. The February winds idly blew scraps of
paper down the empty Detroit streets. The great bronze doors
of the banks were shut. Many would never open again. There
was nothing Frank Murphy or anyone could do about it. The
men with the homburg hats and the broadcloth coats talked with
Murphy for twenty minutes or half an hour and then they went
away, shoulders sloping down a little more, steps a little uncertain. The system was broke and neither Frank Murphy nor
anyone else could put it together. That was what I thought as
I got up, glancing back at the departing bankers and moving
into the open enclosure to talk with Frank Murphy about his
problem, which was, of course, the problem of the country.
That was 1933.

None of us remember the Civil War. We have heard what
it was like. We know that it was the greatest conflict the country has survived (just as we know that it did not resolve many
of the problems which led to its outbreak and that many of the
same problems, in slightly altered form, remain to this day and
constitute the core of our critical contemporary crises: race,
poverty, cultural contradictions).

Younger Americans have no connection with the Civil War
outside of history books, sociological studies, *Gone With the
Wind,* the romanticization of the deadly, dreary, atrocity-spat-
tered war. (My Lai was not the first slaughter of civilians by
U.S. troops.) A handful are familiar with D. W. Griffith's racist
romanticism in *The Birth of a Nation,* but far more have only
heard it debated or have viewed it as an artifact from the
Museum of Modern Art collection. Some may think they evoke
the spirit of the War by waving Confederate flags and stomping

when the band plays "Dixie." But we can only fantasize the feelings of the Civil War. When I was a youngster that was not so. My old uncle, the one who was a little dotty, my father's uncle, really, who held me on his lap and taught me to read, pointing out the newspaper headlines letter by letter, fought in the Civil War. He was a mild, meek man and even at five or six I understood that there was something broken inside of him, something that did not really work any more. But it was only later that I understood that the war had done this. He had gone with the First Wisconsin Volunteers, at Lincoln's first call, and he had fought at Shiloh and Chancellorsville, I think, and the Bloody Angle, and God knows where else. He had been wounded and finally he was taken prisoner and with tens of thousands of other young men in dirty ragged blue thrust into Andersonville. He was one of those who survived. But, of course, only part of him survived. Something had been left back with the pest-holes, the fever wards, the straw pallets, the rats, the stench, the starvation, the scurvy (he lost all his teeth). He was a mild, sweet man and he never talked of Andersonville. I don't think the survivors did. Any more than the survivors of Belsen or Kolyma, or, I suppose, for that matter, My Lai. But you could not look in his eyes without seeing the cloudy veil, that shroud that dulls all perception and permits a remnant of the human spirit to survive such horror.

I have talked to a woman who was a little girl in Georgia when Sherman marched through and who stood in the dust beside the road and watched the old house go up in flames, and heard the squeal of the pigs as their throats were slit and the stillness that followed the quick volley of rifle shots behind the barn, and later saw the twisted body that lay tangled there after the Union riders passed along, the body of her fourteen-year-old brother. The Civil War was blood and terror, hate and death, and it marched from one end of the land to another.

As the war wore on the tattered stream of men slowly

hobbled back to Prairie du Chien, Wisconsin, to Stillwater, Minnesta, to Goshen, Connecticut, to Benton Harbor, Michigan, to Oneida, New York, to Calais, Maine. They limped back to dirt-floored cabins and tried with twisted backs to get in a little corn on the creek bottom so that winter's frost would not bring starvation. That was 1865.

That was the kind of war it was and don't let the figures fool you. We have had nothing like it. The Revolutionary War was not that bad. We came close to destroying ourselves in those days and Appomattox did not end it. In many ways the human questions, the race questions, the ethical questions, the principles over which that war was fought still lie, sometimes much less than skin deep, below the issues that are rending our late twentieth-century America into fragments.

Can we then compare our times with those of the Civil War, with the great quarrel which shattered our nation a little more than 100 years ago? Not in spirit, clearly. For in that quarrel there was deep certainty of right and wrong; a national debate which, in one form or another, had raged for a half a century; massive movements, dedicated with fierce passion, to programmatic principles, leaders with tongues of silver and the lungs of bulls. The North knew where it stood. The South knew where it stood. Within each camp lay extreme views—outriding fringes. There might be doubt as to the Union. But there was no doubt as to where a man stood. It was Right against Wrong but one man's right was another's wrong. There was a sureness, a certainty about goals, about good and evil, which is absent from today. Men swore by their convictions even when brother was pitted against brother. And until the Great Powers (England, France, and Russia) began to nose around the edges of the conflict, it was an all-American dispute; no foreign issues; each side certain that its side was more American than the other.

Today's crisis reflects both cataclysms of the past—of 1861 and 1929. It possesses the force and violence of '61 and the deep pessimism and disillusion of '29. And it has, of course, qualities all its own. We have come to this moment because not only is our social and political system under challenge. We are even in doubt as to the survival of the world we live in. For the first time because of the range and thrust of science we can conceive of the extinction of humanity and we can identify the elements which may bring extinction about. No longer does it seem implausible that our way of life, the structure of our society, can be wiped out or transformed. We know that it can. Societies do rise, decline, transform themselves, rearrange their relationships. The British Empire has fallen in our day. The American Empire may follow in its path. We now begin to see that we could actually destroy ourselves and the world in struggle over the nature of change.

Underlying our debate there is a kind of doomsday psychology. The issues which we are arguing are so profound that we cannot rule out the possibility that we may not survive their resolution.

There is logical reason for every American citizen today to despair and doubt. We have killed one president, compelled a second to retire from office, and the fate of a third is in doubt. Only a dolt would try to whistle through the graveyard of crippled hopes which makes the American dream seem like a bitter joke to so many today. We make war in the name of "peace"; we kill in order to "protect"; we destroy the city, as we say, because it is the only way to save it; we call for reason but speak in the tongues of madness; we call for domestic tranquillity in voices ever louder and rhetoric more and more debased.

Where is hope to be found? It seems to me that it is not to be found in wallpapering our differences, in Pollyannaing the despair, in conning ourselves that "things are not so bad," that we should "accentuate the positive." We are a long way past that.

If hope is to be found it must be found within ourselves; in a perception of the real nature of our times; the real nature of our troubles; an understanding of why so many are so disillusioned, so dissatisfied, so tortured; an understanding of where we stand today and how we got here; of what went wrong and what can make it right; of why some take to the streets and others to heroin; of why some of the young see in the old their deadly enemy; of why some parents see their children—or other people's children—as monsters; of why some Americans see others as faceless villains; why some see danger in the Kremlin and others plant bombs in police stations.

In short, if there is to be any map to the future, we must first discover the point from which we started and then, perhaps, we can trace out a route to where we would like to go. Perhaps, as not a few of us still secretly believe, we can not only save ourselves but build a new and better order for mankind.

Those are the questions which, in, I'm afraid, a discursive fashion, I propose to examine in the following pages.

CHAPTER 2

The Flag Is in Trouble

Where shall we start in the effort to see where we are at in these upside-down, back-to-front, inside-out times? I suppose we might as well begin with ABC's. There has been a lot of talk lately about the flag. The flag is in trouble and this, if nothing else, is as clear a sign as we need of the intensity of the crisis which grips our country.

To me and I think to many others this is a real shocker. I am an old-fashioned man. I love the American flag, love to see it flying, get a thrill out of the colors although for many years I have been much too sophisticated to let on to that. This is George M. Cohan stuff; square. I admit it.

But, of course, that is what the flag is about, for it has no meaning whatever except as the symbol of the country which it represents. When we fight to possess the flag, we are fighting, in truth, for the soul of the country. Today, the flag is no longer the very sign of unity, of oneness, of the Americanness of us all. There are those who cringe when they see the decal on the car window and others who wave the flag violently in the face of their opponents. There are those who hoist it upside down and those who make of it a designer's mod toy.

It was not always so. I remember being at Poltava in the Ukraine in June, 1944, when the first American shuttle bombers flew in from Italy, having hit Rumania en route, to land on Soviet soil. Only a few Americans were on hand to greet the Flying Fortresses, B-17's, the mightiest of their day, but General Ira C. Eaker was received by Russian commanders under the American flag, brightly flying in the stiff Ukrainian breeze. I suppose it is mawkish and sentimental but I can still feel the emotion that choked my throat in that moment. It was a great day for the flag.

When I was a child in Minneapolis, my father got me up at 5:30 A.M., never later than six, on Memorial Day and the Fourth of July. In the stillness of the not-yet-awakened morning, with the sun just slanting through the tall elms outside, we tiptoed up to the attic, dusty, cobwebbed, with its smell of old furniture, medicines from my grandfather's medical cabinets, mothballs, moldering leather, ancient papers. We would rummage back into a dark cubbyhole and carefully pull out the great flag on its heavy oak pole. This we would carry, myself holding the brass-bound end, into the front attic room. We pried open the small window—it was always jammed—then we carefully projected the pole out the window, setting it to fit snugly and securely into the iron stanchion on the floor. After we unfurled the flag I ran down the back staircase into the alley and around to the front of the house to see how it looked. It looked splendid! It always did.

It was the regret of my childhood that we had no small brass cannon, like that in *The Swiss Family Robinson*, to salute the flag. It was another regret that we had no flagpole on the lawn as did some of our neighbors.

During Liberty Loan parades in World War I, in which, as a schoolboy, I participated proudly, it was intoxicating to be one of the multitude that carried the great outspread flag down the center of Nicollet Avenue receiving the tossed silver dollars, quarters, dimes, and even crumpled blanket-style dollar bills. On Arbor Day parades I proudly marched as color guard, shoulder-to-shoulder with my classmate Isadore Pass, who had the honor of carrying the flag because his grades were all A's and my report card showed two or three B's.

The radiator of our 1916 Studebaker boasted a receptacle for the flag. On patriotic holidays or any other day when I could persuade my father, we unfurled a miniature silk flag with a fringe of gold and flew it proudly as we chugged through the streets out into the nearby countryside to the inevitable flat tire, blowout, and breakdown which was the climax of each holiday excursion.

The salute to the flag (I believe it was invented in World War I and there have been some changes in its wording since), was then a simple, heartfelt experience with no posturing, no legionnairisms, no clasping of hand over heart, no touching up, just holding ourselves as straight at attention as small boys' spines could do and the explosive ring-out: "One nation, *indivisible*, with *liberty* and *justice* for *all!*" We shouted it. And at the end we flung our hand out to the flag. Our chests throbbed. We believed it. I still do. Profoundly. Which is not to say that the flag and the love of country which it symbolizes were not vilely distorted in World War I. Within the city of Minneapolis where I grew up, we, myself as a child among hate-sodden adults, turned savagely upon all who believed differently from ourselves. We used the flag as a vehicle of our intolerance just as some do today.

I was born and raised in a patriotic, chauvinistic, Bull Moose Republican family. I supported Teddy Roosevelt with his Big Stick and Manifest Destiny, his bully-for-you, Rough Rider nationalism with all my heart. I grew up looking at the map of the world (all red for the Empire on which the Sun Never Set), longing that it could be all green like the United States. Ameri-

cans were better than anyone else. The doctrine was unquestioned. White Americans, I suppose, although blacks were so few
in my growing up that we children counted their favor a special
privilege. It was different, of course, with Indians. There *were*
many Indians on the streets downtown, particularly at the onset
of winter, and I was raised on the frontier doctrine that "the only
good Indian is a dead Indian."

At the age of seven I was all for war (World War I) and
wore a Charles Evans Hughes button (although really I supported T.R.). I zealously proclaimed Woodrow Wilson a "yellow
dog" because he "promised to keep us out of war" and I was for
fighting side-by-side with the gallant English Tommies and
French Poilus to revenge the poor children of Belgium, their
hands chopped off by the Kaiser's Uhlans. When we entered the
war I hated the "pros"—a "pro" being a pro-German. You didn't
have to use the full phrase. Everyone knew what a "pro" was.
The "good Germans" whom you could not quite trust, changed
their names or said they wished they could. The German con-
ductor of the symphony orchestra was driven from his post;
pacifist and antiwar candidates like the father of Charles A.
Lindbergh were rotten-egged, tarred-and-feathered, ridden out
of town, and worse. Ordinary Germans were made to "kiss the
flag" and mumble patriotic oaths. Not that this won them acceptance. Their saloons were emptied, their stores boycotted,
even the most wondrous store in town, Holtzerman's German toy
shop.

When the war was over the KKK came in. Not against the
blacks. There were not enough of them to make a credible target.
Against the Catholics, mostly, and to a lesser extent, against the
small Jewish community. But mostly, of course, against anyone
who was disliked, who did not conform, or who had the savage
misfortune to get in their way.

It was very thrilling and very patriotic and my schoolmates

and I secretly chalked KKK on the slattern fences of the alleys through which we walked to school. Later on, in the early days of Prohibition, we scrawled the initials BYOL, too. But it was a long time before we learned what those initials meant.

The KKK rode under the flag. No Confederate banner in those days. Certainly not in the North. The fire and brimstone still smoldered and any northern political candidate in trouble "waved the bloody shirt" just as southern demagogues "hollered nigger" (and still do). Late as it was, the Civil War veterans were an honored and respected element in northern society. They were the GAR, the Grand Army of the Republic, a name to thrill a boy's bones. No amorphous catchall "veterans organization." No tawdry drunks. No raucous conventions. No bonus and pension cadgers. The original undiluted Grand Army of the Republic. The "boys in blue" who saved the Union. My heroes. Everybody's heroes. Memorial Day was their day and theirs alone. My old great-uncle, the survivor of Andersonville, tottered down to Nicollet Avenue each May 30 with his fellow survivors and the fine line of men in blue swept up the avenue, flags flying bravely, uniforms worn but neat, whiskers and moustaches white and flourishing, steps firm on that day. But soon the number of marchers began to dwindle and more and more rode—not marched—up the avenue. The GAR marched to "Old Glory" and "The Battle Hymn of the Republic" and my eyes watered at the sight, my heart beat faster, and my sorrow was that I had not been old enough, at least, to have been a Union drummerboy like those in the Oliver Trowbridge books I devoured on long summer afternoons.

The flag was all-embracing. Unimpeachable. The IWW agitators (it was years before I learned that the initials did not actually mean "I Won't Work!") who stood on soapboxes in Gateway Square and harangued the hoboes, the transient workers who harvested the wheat, felled the timber, worked the mines, and maintained the railroads of those days, preached their cause under the flag. So did the Salvation Army and the Volunteers of America. So did the Prohibitionists and the Suffragettes and the disciples of every strange faith who wandered into the city. When radicals marched on May Day, when Union men assembled on Labor Day, when Bohemian immigrants gathered for their annual picnic in Hiawatha Park, they gathered under the flag.

The flag was not lightly used. The rules for its display were strict. No legions of toughs wrapped themselves in flags as a protection or distinction for making cause against fellow Americans. No radicals or iconoclasts carved the flag into odd patterns or embraced some strange device to set themselves apart. The red flag might appear. But it flew beside the Stars and Stripes, proud, no doubt, to be in such company.

All of which is by way of making clear my dissent from those who employ the flag as a symbol of *their* particularity—whatever the nature of that particularity. The flag is our country. God knows we are, always have been, and hopefully always will be a nation of diversity. In that is our strength. But we must have a symbol under which we can all rally. If we now take *the* symbol, the epitome of that America which in the words of the pledge is "one nation, indivisible, with liberty and justice for all," if we take this symbol and make of it an antisymbol, on the one hand, or, on the other, a symbol of pseudopatriotism, of a flaunted, better, higher patriotism than that of our neighbors, or of a cause which exploits the *divisibility* of America and proclaims liberty for some and justice only as a few understand it—then we do, indeed, fall victim to national schizophrenia, tearing at the very core of our being, wounding all, twisting and distorting all that is dear, in greater or lesser measure, to the hearts of flag-bearers and anti-flag-bearers alike.

I do not take lightly those who spurn the flag or those who seek to make of it a protective shield to conceal hatred and ignorance of the principles for which it stands.

It was said, I think, by Dr. Johnson that "patriotism is the last refuge of the scoundrel." This may well be true. Sinclair Lewis aptly predicted in *It Can't Happen Here* that if fascism came to America it would come wrapped in the flag and whistling "The Stars and Stripes Forever."

I do not believe this will happen. If it should we will only deserve it because of our own lack of love for our country, failure to believe in the principles to which we offer lip service, abandonment of those privileges and responsibilities on which the nation is founded, unwillingness to sacrifice our property, time, convenience, or, in the last analysis, our lives for what we think we believe and say we hold dear.

If the flag should become in America a symbol of that tyranny which the republic was founded to oppose, of those who forget or do not believe in the principles of the American Revolution (how many now realize that the Stars and Stripes is the very emblem of Revolution, the oldest, most honored revolutionary banner in existence, long antedating the Johnny-come-lately red flag?), who reject the dream which for a century or more made the Statue of Liberty the beacon of world hope—then this would truly mean that we as Americans had lost our will and our faith in what America is all about.

The flag is not to be cheapened. It is not an advertising trademark to be used to peddle gasoline, a premium to promote magazine sales, a decal of cheap emotion or anti-Americanism. The flag is all of us. To diminish it is to diminish America and in so doing we diminish each of us as an American.

The first sign that the flag was in trouble came not when the New York hard hats used it as a wraparound when they rampaged through the streets, beating up anyone not sporting a butch haircut or an enameled flag in his buttonhole. Nor was the first sign of trouble the mawkish flaunting of Viet Cong banners by antiwar demonstrators or the plaintive act of that Long Island housewife

who, despairing of the war ever ending, began to fly her flag upside down, in the international distress signal.

The first sign came far earlier. It came when Jasper Johns
began to carve the flag into bits and pieces or paint it meticu-
lously as the background of his canvases, when decorator de-
signers laminated the stars and bars on the plastic backs of chairs
and used them for silk-screened walls, when Seventh Avenue
adopted the flag as a thing of chic, cutting it into scarfs, miniskirts, and raincoats.

Don't misunderstand me. I am not suggesting that Jasper
Johns, the pop artists, the profit-eager Seventh Avenue manufac-
turers had any notion of desecrating the flag. They did not. And
that is why the trouble runs so deep. Long since to too many the
flag has been desymbolized, dehydrated, desiccated. Like a trademark we have seen since childhood it is no longer visible, political
significance squeezed out, emotional values drained.

This did not happen overnight. It was not Vietnam that did
it. It was a gradual process like a slow leak in a tire. We are not
suddenly going to restore the flag any more than we are suddenly
going to create national unity by decree or by a spate of Fourth of
July oratory.

But we can take a few honorable steps. We can return to the
code of the flag—to display it only on national and patriotic oc-
casions; to raise it only at sunrise and take it in at sundown (I
must honestly say I don't at all agree with the discovery by the
White House that it's OK to fly the flag all night if there's a spot-
light on it. I grew up to believe that the flag flies all night only
in battle and I see no reason to change a tradition so fundamental,
patriotic, and glorious); to protect it from debasement as an advertising sticker or boxtop premium; to halt its use and misuse by
cliques and factions; to insist that the flag be the banner of all,
rather than the pennant of a few.

But we should not kid ourselves. Until we begin to feel that we are one nation again, until we begin to feel that America is a concept and an ideal for which each may work in his own way, no pious exhortations, no codes, no laws, no moralizing will rally us all behind the Stars and Stripes. The flag's trouble is a symptom. Not the disease. The flag is in trouble because we are all in trouble.

CHAPTER 3

Father Knows Best

One of the things which disturbs many people these days is the challenge to authority which we see everywhere—college students telling college presidents where to get off, priests telling their bishops where to head in, sons and daughters telling their bewildered parents that everything they say and think and feel is obsolete.

Challenge to authority is the hallmark of our times. I do not know precisely what has produced this challenge—a challenge so universal that we find on the one hand the Chinese Red Guards overthrowing their party elders and, on the other, young Dutch iconoclasts, mocking hierarchical Dutch society by forming an antipolitical movement which has begun to win elections. Any social panorama which stretches from the U.S.A. to Peking via Rotterdam merits all the attention we can give it (more on this later).

To look at what is happening in the more narrow context of the American scene I would like to investigate the extent to which we as members of the most advanced technological society are still held prisoner by the myth of superior knowledge. To put it in apple pie terms, one American generation after another has been brought up on the theory that Mom and Dad know best

The Father knows best. Or the Sister. Teacher knows best. Our Elders know best. This shibboleth, of course, is not unique to the United States. It has roots deep in human experience. The elders have always been the holders of the myth, the continuators of the legend, the priests of the sacred fire.

For millennia it was this tradition which preserved the human race by transmitting from one generation to the next the heritage of Knowledge and Experience acquired in the past.

Now, we have passed through the Age of Superstition, the Age of Mysticism, the Age of Belief, the Age of Reason, to enter the Age of Science, and we live in the Era of Expertise in which knowledge is passed on by a computerized technology and mass education. But all we have done is recast the old legend into a new mold. No more High Priests or Magi. OK. But for this pragmatic age we have produced men whom we are told possess the truth—scientific, refined, purified, weighted, balanced, absolute; truth expressed in decimals, percentiles, charts, statistics, theorems, frequency counts. Truth Quantified.

We poor mortals are assured that we cannot expect to reach such heights. We are what we are—fashioned of poor if honest clay, busy with workaday pursuits, earning our livings, studying in our schools, doing our thing, bringing up our families, worrying about the bills and why Johnny stays out too late at night.

We have been conditioned to think that we have neither time nor trained skills to understand such problems as the workings of the Kremlin, the nature of the Communist Conspiracy, the politics of Southeast Asia, the mechanism of the Intercontinental Ballistic Missile, Nuclear Fission (and Fusion), or even the electronic computer, and there are many in high places who comfortably tell us that we are right not to trouble our heads with these matters. Do the theories of the Radical Left and the Radical Right confuse us? Are we too busy trying to stretch our pay checks to understand, for example, the relationship of an "incomes" policy to inflation? Don't worry. The experts have these arcane matters all in hand. Have another beer. Turn on the tube. Relax.

That advice is only too easy to take, for we live in times in which it is not only difficult to understand what is happening, it is difficult to determine what our personal role should be even if we think we know what is going on. There is no point in denying the reality. These are complex days. We have entered what Zbigniew Brzezinski calls the "technotronic era" and we are not going to escape the complexities. But in our attitude toward them lies, I believe, the essence of what we loosely call the "generation gap." Many young people (with the encouragement of some of their elders) challenge the idea that the game is so complicated we can't participate, that we must throw in our hand and leave it all to the experts. In fact, they challenge the validity of almost all of our assumptions and when we try to argue, try to win them back to traditional beliefs, try to overcome their skepticism, we find deep inside ourselves sickly doubts developing. We discover that we are not as certain of those traditions as we thought, and while we may not be ready to follow our children into across-the-board rejection of conventional wisdom and try to conceal our qualms with rage and rhetoric, we are left with the queasy feeling that there may be more truth in the indictment than we publicly will admit.

The roots of the problem are worth digging out.

What is the principal component of the current doctrine of "superior knowledge"? In large measure it consists of the bland reassurances of one set of Washington politicians after another that there exists in the world a genuine font of pure wisdom, that they are, in truth, guided by "men in white," dedicated political scientists, intelligence specialists, defense counsels, economists, prepared to make any sacrifice for the sake of the national interest.

The picture is presented of Washington, struggling with a problem on which the fate of the world as well as our puny existence may hang—the Cuban missile crisis, the Bay of Pigs, the invasion of Cambodia. Thank God, we say, piously, *we* don't have to make the decision. But, thank God, too, that our President has recourse to "information not available to ordinary persons," "secret intelligence data," the recommendations of the "experts," the computer-fed print-outs of the C.I.A., the combined wisdom of the "Joint Chiefs." We do not know exactly who the Joint Chiefs are. We could not name them if our lives depended on it. But they represent to most of us the true continuators of the Delphic Oracles and it is to them that the President turns in hours of crisis for the utter and final refinement of wisdom and knowledge. They are the Elders of the Elders. If they do not know the answers then God Save the Country.

So runs the popular doctrine of superior wisdom. The Greeks would have called it the Doctrine of Sacred Knowledge. The African tribes would have called it voodoo. The Druids called it Magic.

Magic? Voodoo? Wisdom? Expertise?

This is where the younger generation comes in. They don't buy twentieth-century voodoo. They reject it out of hand. They throw a lot of examples at us but since the young are sloppy on their homework it's hard to feel convinced. Yet, we are not going to get very far in exploring today's crisis unless we find a way of making our own judgments, of recognizing the difference between illusion and the real world, of measuring the ability of the modern-day magicians, of understanding whether we are looking out a window or into a mirror.

There is no easy exit from this hang-up but one thing can be done. We can match the experts against the record of history. We can match forecast against performance and discover whether, in fact, superior wisdom exists.

In this exercise let us for a starter put the Vietnam war more or less off limits. It is still on. It is too near, too embarrasing. Just to list the forecasts, analyses, prognostications, predictions, assessments of the elders on Vietnam would take thousands of lines.

Not one has come true. We can argue causes. We can assess blame from Moscow and Peking to the Pentagon, from the jungles of Cambodia to the campuses of the U.S.A. But the result is irrefutable. Hardly one judgment on the war, its end, or the results of our policy has paid off.

Fortunately, the record of the experts in other areas is easily available for analysis. We know the answers about World War II now. All the returns are in. No chance of a cover-up. So how did the Wise Men fare?

First, look at the expert judgments brought in on the eve of World War II:

The Munich Agreement means Peace in Our Time. (It lasted less than a year.)

France has the best land army in Europe. It can't be defeated. (The French Army folded like an accordion; the Germans smashed it in three weeks.)

The Maginot Line is impregnable; the Germans will never repeat 1914. (The Nazi panzers cut through the Maginot Line like butter.)

Never will Nazi Germany and Communist Russia come together. (The Nazi-Soviet Pact kicked off World War II.)

Opinions after World War II started:

The Soviet-German alliance will last 1,000 years. (It lasted twenty-two months.)

The German *Luftwaffe* is the best in Europe; it will squash the British. (The RAF fought the Nazis to a standstill in the Battle of Britain.)

The Nazi panzers are invincible. (The Russians stopped them at Moscow in October, 1941, smashed them at Stalingrad in December, 1942.)

Russia cannot resist the German blitzkrieg; the war will be over in a month or six weeks; Hitler calculated sixty days. (The Russians lost half their country and 20,000,000 men but crushed Hitler.)

These were the basic premises of the military and diplomats on which policy was made. They were shared universally by heads of state and their advisers. Each involves gross misjudgment. Bad as they are they do not match the colossal errors of Hitler or the blunders of Stalin and Roosevelt.

Consider this. Stalin received thousands of intelligence reports telling him that Hitler was going to attack Russia. He was given the day, the date, the hour, the disposition of forces, the German order of battle, the Nazi objectives, the Hitler timetable. He disregarded all. Even after the Germans attacked he would not believe that war was on.

Roosevelt knew that Japan was preparing for war because U.S. intelligence had broken the Japanese code. The news that Pearl Harbor was to be attacked came into Washington several hours before the strike. But fumbling bureaucracy (on a Sunday morning) delayed delivery of the information until too late to warn the Pacific command.

This, incidentally, is another hazard in relying on Superior Wisdom. So often the critical information doesn't get to the top. Intelligence and expertise has reached such mammoth proportions that almost everything in the world is known to someone in every government at any given moment. But to refine, decode, analyze, and get the facts to the decision-maker is a problem no nearer solution than in the days of Louis XIV. Even when the information is on the desk of a Hitler, a Churchill, a Johnson, or a Nixon—will he base his decision on the facts or on some personal hunch?

Prejudice, ignorance, and wishful thinking—these are more constant companions of the "higher authorities" than the information bank and the superior wisdom which is conjured into our minds by the propaganda machine. And this, too, can easily be shown from the record.

Item: The United States perfected the atom bomb in 1945. The *minimum* estimate by the experts of the time it would take the Soviet Union to duplicate the bomb was ten years. The *average* estimate was fifteen to twenty-five years. Many believed that Russia could *never* duplicate it. Russia tested its first A-bomb in October, 1949. It took the Soviets a little more than four years to match Hiroshima.

So rapid was the Soviet advance that she carried out her first test of a hydrogen device in 1953, some months before the United States.

Item: The Russians perfected their Intercontinental Ballistic Missile and lofted their first sputnik in 1957; both events caught the United States flat-footed. The Russians had told American and other scientists about Sputnik nearly ten months before the event but nobody paid attention.

Item: When the Russians halted their nuclear aid program to China in 1958 it was estimated that China would not produce the A-bomb in this century. China carried out her first nuclear test in 1964. She carried out her first H-bomb test in 1967. Early in 1970 she sent her first satellite into space.

Item: When I reported in 1959 that Russia and China had fallen out, top government specialists pooh-poohed the idea; no real clash between Communist powers could occur because they shared a common ideology—that was what the experts said. Within three years the world Communist movement had fallen apart. By the end of the decade war between Russia and China emerged as a strong possibility.

No need to clutter the record. The truth is that the world is so complex, human motivations so complicated, political preju- dices so fierce, that the concept of "expertise" or "superior knowl- edge" as motivating great decisions is, in the classic word of the late Henry L. Mencken, bunk. Any time a serious inquiry is made into high-level deliberations, it discloses that the expertise either is ignored, presents a conflicting or unresolved picture, or is simply wrong.

In the deliberations which preceded President Johnson's decision to bomb North Vietnam, not one specialist on Indochina was called in; not one man with expertise in strategic bombing potentials (that is, with expert knowledge of the classic postwar Strategic Bombing Survey which revealed the failure of strategic bombing against Nazi Germany) participated. The decision was based on politics, politics of the war in Saigon and of the campaign in the U.S.A. Only one person raised the question of what would happen if Hanoi did not sue for peace after six weeks of bombing. The answer was, Then we bomb for another six weeks. Not one man asked what we did if Hanoi held out after the second six weeks. The two six-week periods ended in April, 1966. The question of what to do next was still open four years later.

A study by George F. Kennan of President Wilson's decisions at the time of the Bolshevik Revolution of 1917 shows that not one was made on the basis of the real situation. In each case Wilson either had no reports of what had happened or acted on false or mistaken reports which were the exact opposite of reality.

The "expertise" on which the President, the Secretary of State, or the Secretary of Defense supposedly rely for decisions does not represent actual facts but compromises among competing agencies (for example, the CIA may estimate that there are 25,000 VC in Cambodia; Army intelligence at Saigon offers a figure of 100,000; as a compromise the agreed estimate is 50,000 but no one, CIA, Army, or State, believes in this figure). Or it could be ploys by bureaucratic politicians, or deliberate efforts to "give the President what he wants," regardless of facts and reality.

The modern counterparts of the ancient priesthood are not, on balance, as wise or influential as the oracles of Delphi. They are, at best, sincere, earnest, learned. But, in the end, judgments are human. The data which they present for decision is refined through the personality of the man who submits it and again by the personality of the man to whom it is submitted. Presidents are human. Probably the most human Americans of all. They see the world through their own eyes and they make decisions in terms of

their own needs, their own political careers, their own views of
the world and their roles in it, no matter how statesmanlike they
try to be. They, more than most men, are conscious of their
"image," cognizant of their role in history, eager to appear de-
cisive, successful, imposing, impressive, forceful, vigorous, strong,
and, of course, wise.

The world is a tangle and a web. It is more tangled and more
of a web for Americans than ever before because we are involved
in every part of it and regard ourselves and our success as a sum
of successes not only within our own country but in the most remote regions—the Congo, the bazaars of Lebanon, the fastnesses
of northern Iran, the coral islands of the far Pacific, the cobbled
cities of the Rhine, and the jungles of Indochina.

The American president whoever he may be needs all the
help he can get. So do we ordinary citizens. We need experts and
expertise as never before. But neither we nor the President can
afford to suspend personal judgment and the exercise of common
sense. John F. Kennedy felt that the great lesson he learned from
the Bay of Pigs was, Don't trust the experts—especially don't
trust the military experts. Too often wishful thinking and in-
stitutional loyalty tips the balance.

The experts may know more than you or I. But this must be
proved in each given instance. There is no evidence to show that
their judgment is better than that of the ordinary man or woman
in Des Moines, Iowa, the student at the University of Colorado,
or the struggling blacks of Bedford-Stuyvesant. The "superior
judgment," the "superior wisdom," may just be a cover for bureaucratic rivalry or plain Boston ward politics.

The modern priesthood has attempted to systematize its view
of the world and its problems. It has evolved elaborate systems of
"game theory" in an effort to bring order into the natural chaos
of man and his environment. "Game theory" is particularly attractive to military minds because "war games" have long been part
of command training. To the military, "game theory" is merely an

extension of military exercises to the wide, wide world. One should not denigrate game theory *a priori*. The world is a construct of action-reaction-action. Insofar as decisions are made by men who are similarly conditioned and motivated—who react in accordance with known limits of certainty or uncertainty—game theory works. (It is probably no accident that war games originated with the Prussian army, but the disastrous defeats of Germany in World War I and World War II do not suggest that success in war games means success in war.) It is possible to reduce the whole of life to a slightly complex game of chess or parcheesi. But most of us find it hard to predict with certainty what we will do tomorrow night, let alone what national policy will be after a rapid, dramatic, and unexpected sequence of international events. Game theories are no good if you cannot accurately postulate the bounds of response likely or possible from a given opponent. If Herman Kahn is playing Herman Kahn the game will have a high degree of credibility. It is possible to establish a coefficient which is meaningful in a game between Herman Kahn and Lyndon Johnson. But if Harry Truman is playing Josef Stalin the outcome is likely to astound them both (as it did in Korea). If Herman Kahn is playing Mao Tse-tung (as postulated by Herman Kahn) the game will only be as good as Kahn's imagination is capable of simulating Mao's role. It would be hard to make book on that kind of game and that, alas, is the real game of the world.

For many years when I returned from long trips to the Soviet Union "intelligence" specialists of the U.S. Army, the CIA, or the Air Force would seek me out to try to get some greater reality into their conception of the "enemy." The key question, the one which they always asked with eagerness and pathetic anticipation, was, "Do you have some idea of their timetable?" Or, "What are their priorities?"

Of course, I had no answer for these questions and it did no good to say, as I believed, that "they" (meaning Moscow or Peking or whoever) were not a bunch of electronic buttons on a great computer, all programmed for action with timetables and priorities, but pragmatic, more or less hardheaded politicians, motivated by a range of human factors—ambition, greed, envy, ignorance, power, age, limited knowledge, limited perceptions, weariness—complicated, unsolvable problems at home, a panorama of dangers, perceived and real, abroad, concepts and misconcepts of the U.S. and its intentions, often frustrated as to what to do next and constantly arguing over what the U.S.A. might do.

In other words, the only way to make game theory tell you what the enemy is up to is to locate yourself inside the enemy mind, and even then you will often be bewildered because that is precisely the state he is in: bewilderment.

We have some marvelous experts. They have devoted their lives to studying the Communist world, its strains, stresses, and probabilities. But I have never met a real expert who pretended that he could simulate the reaction response of the other side. If he did claim it—then I knew he was no expert.

Three examples to drive the point home:

When Stalin died no one among our experts (with the single and studiously ignored exception of George Kennan) believed that Soviet policy would change a single degree away from Stalin's terror and hatred of the West. Everyone was wrong, no one more than John Foster Dulles, a classic devotee of systematized thinking.

On the day before it was confirmed that the Russians were putting missiles into Cuba, no expert credited the evidence pouring in. It did not fit their pattern of thinking about Russia; hence it was rejected.

On the day before Khrushchev was dismissed from office by a cabal of his colleagues, not one specialist perceived any hint that this would happen. After the event careful study showed that clear evidence of Khrushchev's slippage had been available for weeks and months. It did not fit the theory; so it was ignored.

The moral: Any time a politician, be he president, secretary

of state, or chairman of the joint chiefs, tells you he has "classified information" that proves a case, expertise that demonstrates
so-and-so, make him lay it on the line. Never forget Mark
Twain's old saying: There are lies, damned lies, and statistics.

The day we begin to abdicate our judgment to Superior Wise
Men in and out of the government is the day we give up the
democratic process and lose control of the judgments on which
the fate of our country and our society depends.

The basis of the challenge of the young is sound. There is
no pool of Superior Wisdom which contains all the answers.
There are no "men in white" whose calculations of world strategy
are surgically precise. We are all of us errant human beings,
some shrewder than others, some luckier than others. Some
have a higher batting average, some a lower. If we are going to
close the "generation gap" we are going to have to ask as sharp
questions as the young. We will have to demand a look at the
options. The world is too complex and too dangerous to make our
bets without knowing the color and value of the hole cards. If, as
Clemenceau said, war is too important to be left to the generals,
national decisions are too important to be left to the politicians,
be they presidents, vice-presidents or even senators. We must all
take a hand. We must make democracy truly participatory.

CHAPTER 4

The Little Old Lady in Tennis Shoes

The little old lady in tennis shoes is right and those like myself who have made fun, felt superior, or found her a comic figure are wrong. Badly wrong.

The Little Old Lady has gone out into the street. She has rung doorbells and distributed literature against fluoridation and sex education classes. She has joined the John Birch Society and she tunes in on H. L. Hunt's Liberty Bell programs. She has given up the comfort of sitting by television and she has dropped out of the bridge club. She may even be neglecting her garden. She has done all this out of concern—concern for her country, concern for its traditions, concern over its enemies, as she perceives them, both internal and external. She is aroused. She is an activist. She is working to save what she believes should be saved and to thwart those whom she believes are dedicated to the destruction of what she holds near and dear.

The little old lady in tennis shoes is no summer soldier. It is a good many years since she first began to fear for her country and she has given without stint of her time, her energy, her emotion, and, quite often, of her money.

She shifts a bit between individuals and between movements. She may now offer her allegiance to Ronald Regan instead of Robert Welch. She may prefer Richard Nixon to Senator Goldwater. But her motivation has hardly changed. She sees her country and her way of life in peril and she has thrown herself into the struggle to preserve and protect it.

People like myself have tended to see her as a figure of the absurd, a slightly ridiculous, quite possibly more than a little obnoxious female Know-Nothing, acting out her frustrations and phobias on a scale of national politics, wooed and readily won by each purveyor of peril, each prophet of doom and disaster, each mountebank of the right (or occasionally of the left), the embodiment of democracy's least attractive aspects.

I have come to believe that view profoundly mistaken. One can, if he will, take issue with the potted analysis of the country's ills which is accepted in good faith by the Little Old Lady. One can, as I do, argue most strenuously with political demagogues who deliberately prey on her terrors, who subvert her natural suspicions and turn them inward against paranoid conspiracy or outward against impending Doomsday.

But one must distinguish between the Little Old Lady and those who seek to use her for their own purposes, usually cynical, often dangerous, and not infrequently pecuniary.

The Little Old Lady is an action-motivated individual. She takes her responsibilities as a citizen of the United States seriously. She has observed the world and finds it filled with danger. She sees the anchors of her faith, the framework into which her life has been poured, rocked by the titanic forces and counterforces of the age, and she has gone out of her home to the barricades, regardless of infirmity and personal comfort. If she is not an altogether admirable character (and who, for that matter, is) she is at least no figure of fun or satire. She is on the firing line and she was the first to get there.

Now, today, of course she has been joined by millions of fellow citizens. Just as she left the comfort of her home to ring doorbells and attend mass meetings so they have thronged out into the political arena. They have joined the long treks to Washington, the mighty assemblages in Central Park or the Boston Common or the Civic Square in San Francisco. They have been tear gassed in Berkeley and clubbed in Chicago. And some have been shot and killed in Kent State or Santa Barbara. In Augusta. Or Jackson. Or Cleveland. Or Chicago.

Politicians, elected politicians, that is, governors, presidents, members of Congress, don't like this—with a few exceptions. It is not playing the game as they learned the game. They see it as dangerous—to them, of course, and that is the way, for the most part, we interpret danger. The other fellow's danger never seems so perilous as that which threatens us.

When politicians in office spot a mass of humanity descending on them, be it grim-faced ladies in tennis shoes, demanding an End to Communism in the Schools, or a leonine throng of young people demanding an End of the War in Vietnam, they become nervous. They are apt to equate the End of Communism or the End of the War with an End to their career in the U.S. Senate or in Congress or the State House.

When politicians are threatened they get up-tight. They shout back, duck, holler cop, try the put-down. So it is that we hear the cry that "The law is not made in the streets," "No mob is going to change our course." When violence results, as it almost always does, there are demands by the Politicians-in-Office that the struggle be carried on "within the system." By which they mean that the concerned citizens abandon the demonstrations, the street action, and utilize the lobby, the telephone, letter-writing, arm-twisting, jawboning, instead of the shouted slogan.

There are two sides to this question as the Little Old Ladies of the left and right and their children have discovered. The reason for taking to direct action, be it ringing doorbells or gathering under the Washington Monument, is not, for the most part, any desire to go outside the system. It is simply a desire to be heard, to get the message across. The shouting and the angry words are caused, plain and simple, by the atrophy of the system itself. The system long since ceased to work for you and me, Little Old Lady, Women's Lib, Young Dissident, Angry Black, Frustrated Blue-Collar, or Gray-Flannel Businessman.

The growing mass action, the doorbell-ringing, the Martin Luther King marches, the encampments in Washington, the taking to the streets by the young, are perceived by the political establishment as a danger, and some of this sense of anxiety is communicated to the public at large, for it, too, has long since outgrown the habits and responsibilities of real democracy.

Politicians are no strangers to political pressures. They live their lives among them. What to them seems strange, unpredictable, and therefore menacing, is the political pressure of the ordinary citizen, concerned about issues, about principles. Politics in the politicians' phrase is a 'game." It is played by the rules. The best players stay in office a long time. They become Speaker of the House, Chairman of the Rules Committee, Director of the Budget. They acquire perquisites of office (and sometimes lots of money), power, chauffeurs, the ability to make ordinary civil servants cringe and quiver. They hold court and are loaded with honors. Lobbyists fawn on them (and arrange exotic outings and, sometimes, exotic young ladies as traveling companions). You will search the Declaration of Independence and the Constitution of the United States in vain for any rules to the "game of politics." The Founding Fathers did not create the "more perfect union" with the game and its players in mind. But, to be sure, not too many of today's players could readily tell you the content either of the Declaration of Independence or of the Constitution. (More than a few citizens are fuzzy on this—some of them so fuzzy that they denounce the Bill of Rights as subversive!)

Over the years politics and government have become a cliché. The New England town meeting (except in a few communities, small and remote) has died out. The tradition of the citizen, concerned, argumentative, deliberative, debating every proposal that affects his life, is as extinct as the dodo. Long since the citizen has abandoned his participation and responsibility, encouraged by the "professionals" to leave such complex matters to them. In the big cities and big states the citizen may not even know his Congressman's name; he never knows his state representative or even who represents him in the city council. Not only does he not know the name, he hasn't the vaguest idea of what his anonymous representative in Washington is doing. If he knows one bill in 100 on which his Congressman has voted it is remarkable. Nor does the politician know many of the ordinary people who, in theory, chose him and who, in theory, he represents. But he probably knows very well and talks every day with the man who actually picked him to run or put up the money for the campaign—the Big Boss of the Machine or possibly the Big Economic Interest of his district.

In place of the individual there have grown up the Big Blocs—Big Business, Big Labor, Big Farming, Big Banking—the special interest cliques. *They* know the Congressmen. The Congressmen know them. What is more important the Congressman's administrative assistants know them.

This is not the way our government is supposed to run. It is not the way we are taught in school. But long since we have ceased to be a democracy as Washington, Jefferson, Hamilton, and Adams conceived a democracy—a government by, for, and of the people. The people today are just a casual ingredient. The weight is swung by Big Interests—the lobbies, the lobbyists (usually ex-Congressmen or ex-bureaucrats or ex-generals). The big interests are not only Big Business but Big Bureaucracy. The government responds quickly to itself, its own internal pressures and interests. It matters little who is in the White House or Congress except as regional or economic emphases may shift—the Pentagon, HEW, Interior, the Corps of Engineers roll right on. Big Business and Big Bureaucracy know each other and, usually, work together. There is a Congressman for Boeing. There is Mr. Banking Interests. There is the Congressman for the Dairy Lobby. For the AFL-CIO. The Congressmen (it takes a multitude to serve them) for Oil. For Big Highways. For Electronic Computers. For ABM's. For ICBM's. For Nuclear Submarines. For the Treasury. And even for the State Department. Of course, here and there is a Congressman who just represents people. Very rare, these.

This is the System. It is not sensitive to individuals. In fact, the System discourages the individual in every way. He is a nuisance or a nut, upsetting delicate arrangements. The System closes ranks against him. Nor does the System recognize citizens in groups unless they happen to fit the existing pattern. If you have a problem there is a recognized way of handling it—through the appropriate lobbyist. If you are having a little trouble with the Justice Department there is a Man to See—quietly, no publicity, a working out of a misunderstanding, no hard feelings you understand, we help you, you help us. That's the way the System handles things. After all, the Politician-in-Office, be he in Congress, the Post Office, or the Pentagon, is a busy man. He is dealing with millions or billions every day. It is a long, long time since he thought of himself as what he really is—an employee of yours and mine. We pay his salary. We (in theory) can hire or fire him. He doesn't like to think of that. He may even have forgotten it. He may think that he has some special right (seniority or superior wisdom) which sets him apart from the Little Old Lady, the kid with the long hair, or the button-down lawyer from Madison Avenue.

The System may not be what brought the Little Old Lady,

the College Youth, the Black, the Button-Down Collar, and the Hard Hat into the streets. But it had more to do with it than anything else.

Because the fact is that today's system has nothing except a few genuflections in common with the system as it was set up by the Founding Fathers.

The Founding Fathers were a great deal more familiar with the democratic process than most of its so-called practitioners today. In fact, they invented it in modern form. They were, for the most part, as Walter Hickel noted, young men. They spent most of their very active lifetimes thinking about government and its problems. Although they belonged largely to an Established Class, they carried out a successful revolution, a real revolution, in which the blood of the people was shed, in which property was destroyed, buildings burned and shelled, men put up against the wall and shot (on both sides), thousands made refugees and driven from the country, the land laid waste—all of this done in a protracted and savage guerrilla war against the greatest power of the day. There was not much about the very revolutionary system of democracy which these young men did not know. They had fought with every bit of energy and intellect at their command to create a system which they put in the place of the King's Writ. They thought the Government of Man was the most important thing in their lives. They did not allot a few minutes a day to ritual repetition of a little meaningless rhetoric. They did not simply switch on the radio, spend three minutes listening to the news bulletins from Washington and Saigon, then turn off their minds. They did not limit their interest in politics to the campaign year or a single issue. They spent weeks, months, years in politics and nothing but politics, because they believed that unless you could fashion an effective means for regulating public affairs nothing else made any difference. The rest of the country agreed with them. If business, commerce, and farming was neglected, if profits vanished, if belts had to be tightened—tough luck. First things first. First, settle the country's business. Then worry about your own. Of course, those were simpler times; we were a largely agricultural homogeneous country. Today's complex technological society presents much more complicated decisions. Yet, the essence of the matter is one of emphasis. Do we put *our* business first? Or the country's? As John F. Kennedy put it, "Ask not what your country can do for you but what you can do for your country."

Some of those who sit in on the participatory democracy of our youth culture suppose it can't be matched for diversity of viewpoint, confusion of thought, conflict of ideas, violence of expression. The young certainly indulge in riots of rhetoric. But go back to the Founding Fathers. True, you find elegance of language—more philosophy, no obscenity. But underlying their debates is the same power, vigor, search for first principles, for hard rocks on which to anchor faith.

You will try in vain to find any corollary between the Federalist Papers, with their pungent, relentless logic, and the puerile palaver which passes for oratory in today's Congress, the flaccid substitute for reason and truth to be found in the hollow rationalizations of the government propagandists.

The Little Old Ladies are right. So are the students. The foundations of the republic are in danger. In fact, some have simply dissolved in the sterile stew of neodemocracy which passes for the real thing in Washington. The politicians are right to feel menaced by the arousal of the citizenry because what the citizens threaten is the whole cozy, comfortable, profitable, nondemocratic, back-scratching system which has grown up—a system that is composed—and only composed—of the National Legislature, the White House, the Great Departments, and the affiliated Lobbies. Ordinary citizens need not apply. If we do write enough letters they are sometimes weighed and given computerized replies. The weight of the pros, cons, and unde-cideds may or may not be taken into account by the Statesman in deciding his next move.

The reason why the Politicians-in-Office fear, resent, and are enraged by a participatory citizenry is that the citizens don't play the game. Why should they? They have no chips in the Big Money lobbies, the huge concrete-and-gasoline companies, the Computer-Defense interests. The citizens have the simplicity and the naïveté to suppose they still live under the system which the Founding Fathers set up. They believe in it. They support it. They fight for it. They challenge the infallibility of the High Priests. They demand simple things: Lower taxes. No bussing. End the war. End the draft. End discrimination. Civil rights. Better schools. High tariffs. Or low.

Very disturbing. Of course, for the most part, the politician in office tries to ignore them. Or criticizes them. Or excoriates them. Or refuses to see them. But there is always that haunting danger that some other politician might be willing to play their game, to make a coalition, to see whether, in fact, it is still possible for democracy to bring results. Or, in another context, to harness them to his own selfish personal interest.

A century and a quarter ago Europe trembled when Karl Marx warned, "A spectre is haunting Europe, the spectre of Communism." Marx was wrong. So were those who thought his prophecy might come true tomorrow. But it is not wrong to say today that a spectre is haunting Washington—the spectre of democracy. The spectre is real. Washington's fear is soundly based. For if the day comes when real democracy returns to Washington it will indeed be a time of change.

When the Eugene McCarthy movement began its quixotic course in December, 1967, Washington snickered and went on to more serious matters. It was only in the last days of New Hampshire that the pros suddenly sensed alarm. Here was something that threatened the whole pattern of rules on which the game of politics was founded. To be sure, they had heard of cases like this in the distant past. William Jennings Bryan and his "free silver" crusade. Teddy Roosevelt and his Bull Moose Party, the radical agrarians of Wisconsin, North Dakota, Minnesota, Father Coughlin in the 1930s, and even Huey Long. But that was long ago. Before modern communications media, publicity techniques, the big money campaign which television had imposed. The idea of a popular crusade seemed to the professionals a joke—a rather bad joke. Of course, there had been some crusade psychology in the first Adlai Stevenson campaign and in the Goldwater campaign. But nothing serious (as the results of 1952 and 1964 made plain).

What was so disconcerting about the McCarthy crusade was that it seemed to *work*. It brought results, won elections, turned over the political situation, set the populace afire. There wasn't a politician in the country who failed to notice this; and not one, quite possibly even including Eugene McCarthy, who really felt comfortable with this phenomenon. For if people took the system into their own hands, no one could be certain of the outcome. The people could put in McCarthy today; but they could remove him tomorrow. King Mob would triumph. Or so it seemed to the habit-bound, antipopular members of the System. That is why since the 1968 election Politicians-in-Office have viewed with such a wary, troubled eye the continuance and growth of popular politics, be it of left, right, or center. For if people keep coming into the streets, if they really get it into their heads that the streets do belong to the people in peaceful assembly, what politician can view the future—his future, of course—with equanimity? Today the people are for the war or against it, for civil rights or against them, for the earth and its survival or against a particular environmental proposal. What will tomorrow bring? It does not occur to the Politician-in-Office, or if so only seldom, that the System does not belong to him, was not created for his benefit, is not some kind of a perpetual social security; it was created for and by the very people whose activities (and views) he deplores. It exists by sufferance of the people. It may at any time be changed by them. That, as the Little Old Ladies long since perceived, is what democracy is all about—participatory democracy, that is, the kind the Founding Fathers practiced, perfected, and bequeathed to us, for better or for worse, for all time.

CHAPTER 5

The Dream of
the Mushroom Cloud

For many years I have lived with the dream of the mushroom cloud. I am not speaking figuratively but literally. Periodically I dream of nuclear war. The dream is vivid and real. The war has started or is about to start. I am in the city, walking down some random street, Third Avenue, for instance, or a side street off Park. The siren sounds. It is the same siren I heard in London during the blitz. It is the same siren I heard in Algiers, in Tunis, in Cairo, in Moscow. No one who has heard the siren will ever forget it. But this time I know it means that nuclear war is starting. There is only a minute to find a place to hide. I run wildly, looking for a doorway, a cellarway, any place to take refuge. Others are running too. Frantically I run from entrance to entrance. This one is too shallow. The next is closed and barred. There is a long blank wall. I run to its end and turn the corner just as the sky lights up with a ghastly light. The bomb!

Of course, there are permutations of the dream. Sometimes, I am walking through a park. I know the siren will sound in an instant. I hurry . . . faster . . . faster . . . faster . . . But there is no escape. I hear the distant rise of the siren and sink to earth, trying to claw myself into it as the bomb's light spreads over the sky. The physical circumstances of this park are familiar to me and real. It is 1943 and I have spent a very late evening in London with Aneurin Bevan and Jennie Lee, talking about the future of the world. It is too late for cabs and I am taking a shortcut across the park in the blackout. Just as I reach the center of an endlessly open meadow, the sirens go and instantly there is the bark of the antiaircraft guns and the crash of the bombs. It is this reality, this actual experience, onto which the dream of the A-bomb is grafted.

How many of us live with the dream of the bomb and for how many years have we so lived! We have seen the picture of the mushroom cloud. We have, some of us, seen the indescribable films of Hiroshima and Nagasaki—the reality of putrefying flesh, fire-glazed eyes, ragged, peeling skin with the bubbles of fat, pus-oozing bodies, the stench (how can it come through the film so rank and rancid you can never get it out of your nostrils?).

We have lived with this terror for a quarter of a century. We dream it periodically. Especially when there is an international crisis and it seems possible that the Day may come. I think we all dream the same dream, except for individual details. We fit the Bomb into the range of our experience. Those who have lived under bombing in one war or another can render the Bomb easily into their imagination. For it is merely the ultimate permutation of the terror with which we lived in England, or in Germany, or in Russia, or more lately in Indochina. The ultimate Terror is like the penultimate, or it is the sum of all the other terrors and we compose in our imagination its image from the smaller terrors of our own lives.

I mention the dream of the mushroom cloud because a theory has gained a certain vogue that what distinguishes the present generation from all other generations (and, thus, makes it separate, nonrelative, and independently reactive) is that this is the first which has lived its whole life in the knowledge that the world could be destroyed in a single instant of nuclear war.

It is, some sociologists say, this doom overhanging us like a projection of Hell described by Dante and pictured by Gustave Doré which has set the world awry—has caused young people to challenge the traditions, the mores, the life-style, the politics, the morals of their elders.

Well, maybe. The human imagination is capable of remarkable feats. Tom Sawyer saw in that single circular window high in the church transept behind the altar the very eye of God, looking down on him in terrible majesty. A whole generation of Victorian children came to maturity believing literally in the torment of Hell, the fire and brimstone, the tortures of the damned, so vividly limned by preacher and book. Sin, they *knew*, meant eternal damnation—torture as vivid as any filmed by putty-faced Japanese Army photographers at Hiroshima.

Did that vision of Hell, the sizzling reality of its fires, the sickening torments of the God Enraged, did that desperate future, so real for a generation of sinners, male and female, color their Weltanschauung? Did it move them to the brink of precipice, ever fearing that one misstep and God, himself, would blow the whistle?

In all fairness I do not think so. Of course, the vision of the Torture of the Damned conditioned minds. But it did not abolish Sin. Indeed, Sin may have reached peaks of intensity in the Victorian era never touched before or since.

But, it can be argued, this was an imaginary terror—even though it may have been a most believed and believable one. What of real terror and its effect on the psyche? We have an example very close at hand—the terror of conventional bombing. It is true that the Nazi blitz against London did not wipe the city from the map. But that is not the way the danger was perceived before the outbreak of war. The world had a foretaste of what to expect. Perhaps, many have now forgotten Barcelona, Guernica, Madrid. But to the world of the '30s these were the harbingers of what the next World War would bring. Look back at the Hearst Sunday supplements, at the evocative articles in *Liberty, Colliers,* the *Saturday Evening Post.* They spelled out what the citizens of the world believed to be the reality of aerial warfare—total destruction, total casualties. London, Paris, Berlin wiped from the face of the earth. Not even New York and Washington were safe. Oh, yes. I know it sounds naïve and unrealistic. It did not sound so in the late '30s. It was very real. I believed it. So did everyone I knew. Civil Defense authorities in England estimated that first-strike casualties would be at least 600,000 killed. That was what they expected on the first wave of Nazi bombing, most of the toll, of course, occurring in London. That was what they tried to prepare for. It was this that gave the emotional force, the political strength to Chamberlain and Daladier, to Munich, to Peace in Our Time. It is so easy to forget what we all thought World War II would bring. But it is what the world feels which determines and conditions an era— the feeling, not the cold scientific facts which the historians later are at such pains to uncover.

Is there a difference in degree between the vision of total destruction by Nazi mass bombardment and the vision of total destruction by the Bomb? Yes. It is true that in 1939 we said "There is no place to hide." But there *was* a place to hide. Switzerland, perhaps. Or Scandinavia. Or, maybe, Buenos Aires. We foresaw only the total obliteration of London. Not the obliteration of the British Isles in one apocalyptic flash. A difference, surely. But is it a critical difference?

Some would say Yes because for the first time the A-bomb and the H-bomb have created a world which cannot survive the use of these weapons. But this is certainly arguable—arguable in the kind of terms which produces no conclusion because if

London is your world and it is destroyed and you along with it, what weight can be given to the fact that, after all, Melbourne and Sydney survive untouched?

Nor is the quantum leap in destructivity which is implied by the Bomb entirely without precedent. What of the world into which gunpowder was introduced? What were the visions which this mysterious, uncontrollable, totally destructive force created? We can, if we wish, go back to the chronicles which describe its first use in China, its superlative effects when introduced into Europe. Or to take a simple and comprehensible example —what happened when gunpowder was introduced by the Spaniards into the New World. The trauma of the victim was total. For generations there was no recovery. Not to this day, in fact. To the victims the men who possessed this power possessed the power to destroy the earth. They were true Gods. Not the sons of Thor but Thor himself, armed with the supernatural thunderbolt which struck down all, destroyed all. After the gods passed by, the world as it had been known was forever gone. The empire of the Incas vanished. So did that of the Aztecs. Here was technology combined with military power in a manner which mankind had not previously seen. The effect upon the morals, mores, and psyche of society was observable and measurable. Is the terror of today as great as the terror of gunpowder? This is no easy question to answer but the fact that it can be raised demonstrates that the Terror of the Atom is not entirely without precedent.

It is true, nonetheless, that the Bomb for the first time confronts us with the genuine prospect that the very world will be destroyed. And this, to us, is what is so new, so shattering. But, even here, we cannot be really certain that mankind has not faced in earlier days the threat of total extinction.

We do not possess a human record of previous global cataclysms, although the imprint of them is clearly embodied in legend and tradition. The most famous of these is the tale of

Noah and the Ark. To be sure, the scientists now believe that
the events referred to in Noah's narrative must have been re-
stricted. It was not the *whole* world which was obliterated by the
deluge. But, at most, only a small portion, perhaps the region of
Mt. Ararat in Asia Minor. But this begs the question. For to
Noah it was *his* world which faced extinction; it was the known
world of those who handed on the legend. It may have been, as
sophisticated scholars insist, only a part of the globe. But the
same argument can be made today. We might say, for instance,
that it is only the earth, a tiny, tiny bit of matter in the vast
universe, which is threatened. But it is *our* world. That is what
counts. Noah's world was wiped out. This is the vision which
threatens us.

We may go further in examining the precedents of total
extinction. We do not know for certain that the world, as a
habitable place, has not been wiped out in the past. We are still
trying to reconstruct the evidence of the ice ages. It seems probable that man in those times also faced the prospect of the
eradication of his known world.

Bring the story down closer to the present day. What of the
barbarians who wiped out Rome and Athens? And, again, Europe,
that is to say, the "known" world of its times, was very nearly
wiped out not once but repeatedly in the fifteenth and sixteenth
centuries. It was not an atom bomb. It was the black death, the
plague. The terror was in a sense more deadly than that of the
Bomb, for man had only the vaguest notion of the enemy which
threatened him. Villages and towns were obliterated. Every man,
woman, and child was destroyed, often in a few days or weeks.
Great cities like London lost three-quarters of their population
overnight. There was no one to bury the dead. Nations were deci-
mated, never to recover. And no one knew from one day to the
next where, when, or whether the destroyer would strike. In
terms of today one would have to contemplate the possibility
that at any moment nuclear war might arise, not from a known

enemy, but from an unknown one. It could strike any city, any region, any country. It could strike on successive days, again and again. Or, by chance, it could pass by and leave a place untouched.

Did this terror traumatize a generation? Probably not. The accounts we have of human existence in the time of the plague reveal too clearly that life went on beside death, in the very jaws of death, as it were.

Of course, it may be that the belief in the universality of the destruction which is implicit in the Bomb has a quality that is more pervasive than any previous horror. But I think this not likely. True, we live with our nightmares. True, when international tension rises the breath of nuclear death quickens. But it is characteristic of human beings to reject, to put out of mind the most awful of possibilities. This is how we survive.

There is even a scientific name for this phenomenon. It is called "denial," or suppression by the mind and the rejection of facts too unpleasant to face. We saw the phenomenon in the Nazi concentration camps during World War II. It was common in the Soviet Union under Stalin. It explains why terminal cancer victims do not kill themselves.

So I conclude that the Bomb is not the chief conditioning factor underlying our crisis. I do not mean that the Bomb does not play a role. Certainly, it gives to many discussions an aura of Apocalypse—a feeling of living in the grasp of forces which we cannot master. But this, of course, is the fundamental condition of man and has been since creation. He has had to learn to live with and command forces vaster than himself from the very beginning. His survival is evidence of his persisting ability to cope, in one way or another, with the greater strength of nature.

No. I think that we will find the root of contemporary social disturbance in the real and the present rather than in the theoretical or possible—that is, in the reality of present war (Vietnam), the reality of race (Panthers vs. Police), the reality of the ecology crisis, the reality of obsolete malfunctioning and distorted political institutions and practices.

A young man is more quickly traumatized by being drafted into a war which he regards as pointless or malevolent (or by fear of the draft) than by dreams of the Bomb. A black is more quickly traumatized by a white officer clubbing a black youngster than by a "Ban the Bomb" poster. A suburban housewife is traumatized when the bulldozer crushes the ancient maples that edge her lawn. A reporter is traumatized by a subpoena calling on him to submit his confidential notes to a grand jury.

The dream of the mushroom cloud adds to our tensions, raises our anxieties. But it is Kent State, Cambodia, Jackson, smog, the Santa Barbara oil slick—that sends the adrenalin into our blood and causes us to wonder where America is going and where we ourselves, young or old, black or white, radical or conservative, or just plain middle-aged, middle-of-the-road, are going to end up.

CHAPTER 6

The Shook-Up World

A little more than ten years ago I got on the subway about 5:30 one afternoon at Times Square and twenty minutes later emerged into an alien world. Not just a neighborhood that was new, although I had never been in Red Hook, Brooklyn, but a world that was different as Russia is from America, or Uganda from Scotland—a world where people lived under different laws, spoke a different language, wore a different dress, worshiped different gods, were educated in a different culture, lived by different values—a world which knew as little of that in which I lived as I did of theirs.

This was the milieu of what I came to call the Shook-Up Generation, the world of the street-fighting or bopping gangs, alienated young people, a world of counter-culture, counter-morals, counter-values.

I want to go back to look at the Shook-Up World again because I think it tells a lot about the world in which we live and the way in which we as individuals and collectively as nations act and react.

In the time when I was standing around on chilly February nights in candy stores or on street corners with the gangs, I often heard social workers suggest that the violence of the young, the mortal dangers of the street, were caused by imitation. The Shook-Up World was imitating adult life and the real world. The teenagers were constructing a violent world in the image of the violent world they saw depicted on the television screen or described in the newspaper headlines—especially the headlines and the graphic pictures of the tabloid *Daily News* and *Mirror*. That, many thought, was the crux of the problem.

At the time I reserved my judgment, but the deeper I got into the Shook-Up World the less I thought of this analysis. Today, in the perspective of a decade in which the world of the streets has changed considerably (it's almost entirely a drug scene now; bopping is as old-fashioned as a zoot suit) and the "real" world has grown more and more violent, I think even less of the notion that the youngsters were emulating their misguided adults. I think something much more fundamental was going on in the streets of New York which bears close study for the clues it gives us to human character and human reactions.

Let's look at what I found when I ventured into the streets of Red Hook. At first, I confess, I could not even understand what the youngsters were saying and my remarks to them were hardly more comprehensible. It was not only that they used a jargon, a street slang, with which I was totally unfamiliar, their conversation dealt with acts and concepts beyond my ken. Just as, had I talked to them about motivation, alienation, democracy, ideology, orientation, credibility, or class consciousness, they would have looked at me blankly or muttered, "Man! You're really gone!"

They lived in a world in which fear and insecurity was institutionalized. To Blood, the sixteen-year-old war minister of a gang which comprised almost all the youngsters between the ages of eight and eighteen in one South Brooklyn Housing project and which called itself the Cobras, there was not one person in the world he trusted outside of his fellow Cobras—no family, no adults, no schoolteacher, no probation officer, no social worker, no priest, no judge, and, of course, no policeman. There was no place where he felt safe. None. He went to sleep late every night (seldom before 1 or 2) in fear, and the first thing he felt in the morning mixed with the raw burn of his hangover was the ugly taste of fear. He awakened every morning with the real and present conviction that he might not live through the day. This was no phobia based on fantasies of the nuclear world. He would not have known a mushroom cloud if he saw one. The fear that he would die before nightfall was based on cold calculation of the odds—he could be killed by a cop (two or three of his friends had been killed by cops in recent months); he could be killed by a rival gang, either in a rumble (a formal gang war) or by being bopped by a lone assassin or a group of thugs as he slithered through the streets to school or to a rendezvous with a friend. Every step he took was dangerous. He might be shot by the corner grocery man as he snatched a melon; he might be run down by the next car that turned into President Street, another bopster at the wheel; he might be ambushed and thrown from the roof of the tenement in which he lived; he might get drunk and be stabbed in the heart by an older drinker for the 75 cents in his pocket; he might be arrested, dragged into detention, there to be killed because he refused to be used by an adult homosexual. There was no end to the dangers in which Blood lived. They were all real, all present. They existed in the building where he lived, in the block where he lived, in the neighborhood where he and his friends had their gang.

There was nothing unique about Blood. His life was lived in duplicate by thousands of other New York teenagers. And not only in New York. In more or less similar circumstances there were thousands of Bloods in every city of any size and (with a few changes of detail) there were thousands more in the smaller towns and in the countryside. Blood was a Puerto Rican. But the bopping gang was not confined to Puerto Ricans. There were black gangs. Irish gangs. Italian gangs. Jewish gangs. There were gangs of mixed nationalities, although not so many. The basis of the gang was not ethnic. It was geographic. Because residence patterns were segregational the gang was dominated by one ethnic group—although exceptions could be found. Some gangs called themselves Lords. Others were Dragons or Cherokees. Some improbably were Bishops. Others were Chaplains. But whatever they called themselves, whatever their ethnic base, their life-style was the same.

The relationship of the gang to the dangers of life was simple and direct. Ask any bopster why he bopped. He thought the question was crazy. Protection, he said. You had to believe him. If you suggested that the gangs imperiled each other's lives with their bloody fatal battles, he shrugged his shoulders. That was life. You had to protect yourself. Against the other gang. That meant fighting. Sure it was dangerous. But in a world of dangers this was simply one more. And there was no escape, for, as one put it, "A Bishop is always a Bishop and a Chaplain is always a Chaplain and there is no such thing as a cool."

The gang was Blood's life. If he had a moment of security, relaxation, or joy it was with fellow gang members. Possibly on a dark winter's afternoon, sharing a bottle of sneaky pete in someone's room, letting the warm glow of the wine blur the dangers lurking outside the door and the hunger growling in his belly.

The gangs operated on a principle of territoriality—"turf," as they called it. Each gang's territory or turf was as precisely designated as a multilateral international treaty delineating the boundaries of great empires. Generally speaking they followed the principle of the thalweg (I wish I had known the word then— it would have broken up Blood and his companions)—that is, the dividing line was presumed to run down the middle of boundary streets with occasional exceptions. Sometimes the exceptions were extraordinarily important—a movie house which "belonged" to one gang but was physically located on the turf of another, a candy store which was the meeting place of the Cobras but could only be reached by crossing the turf of the enemy Apaches or by a roundabout detour. No problem when a "cool" was on. But a *causus belli* when relations between the Cobras and the Apaches were deteriorating toward "war." It was called "war" when it broke out and it followed the rules of adult wars, insofar as these were understood by the juveniles. There were several kinds of war. There was all-out war, in which the Cobras and all their affiliated or "brother" gangs joined in against an opposition coalition. These coalitions, like those of the adult world, were amorphous. Some gangs were permanent partners, some were shifting and uncertain allies. The all-out wars, like world wars, had a tendency to spread and enlarge, embroiling larger and larger areas of the city until regions which had been, perhaps, "cool" for many months suddenly erupted in deadly combat.

Wars often arose suddenly and almost without notice—an obscure wrangle, an attack of uncertain origin or motivation, a fancied insult, a misinterpreted act or gesture, a leader's ambition to prove his masculinity—any of these was enough to fire passions. Usually war broke out between gangs which were territorial neighbors, gangs which had a long record of conflict and enmity, gangs which had fought each other off and on since before any of the present members had been born. One thing quickly became apparent: while the bopping gang had recently proliferated and street warfare had become stylized, it was nothing new. It had been present in New York for at least 125 years and possibly longer. The "gangs of New York" had held sway in whole sections of the nineteenth-century city, where police never entered or only in detachments of force. In fact, if we trace the history of adolescent combat we find that its roots are lost in antiquity. In medieval England the brawny yeoman of one village fought those of the next on Sundays on the green. In Russia today the boys of one town regularly fight those of the next. The street brawls of Glasgow, Liverpool, or Dublin are classic.

The ritual of the bopping gangs differed only in style from the classic contests of rural England or the Russian village. Bopping gangs which were distant from each other and knew each other only by "rep" seldom fought unless a "brother war" occurred. When you tried to get at the root of the trouble, you found, as with nations, that it was difficult to establish warranted facts, that each side had a vision of the other which was hugely distorted by emotion and prejudice; efforts to iron out the trouble often only made it worse. You also found that if gangs had just emerged from a bloody battle they were likely to cool it for a good long time, licking their wounds and trying to recoup their strength.

But there were other kinds of wars than the all-out variety. There was limited war (something like Vietnam or Korea or the Arab-Israel affair), in which each side observed certain understood but definite rules—no bopping, for instance, on the way to or from school, no bopping in the Saturday movie house, no use of zip guns (homemade guns which fired a cartridge with the aid of a rubber-band hammer). Sometimes these conventions were the subject of negotiation. Sometimes they were simply understood. Often, they were violated by one side or another (as in the case of MacArthur's drive to the Yalu or President Nixon's invasion of Cambodia) and limited war suddenly expanded in a violent outburst.

There was also the set battle and the test of champions, two obvious survivals from medieval knighthood improbably flowering in the rubbish lots of Red Hook and the Lower East Side. The set battle was an engagement at a specified time and specified place with specified weapons (car aerials permitted as spears or whips but no switchblades or bicycle chains, combat limited to forty members of each gang, time: 8:30 P.M., place: the locked and cattle-fenced playground of the Benjamin Franklin High School). In theory the set battle ended the quarrel and a cool followed automatically. In reality the agreed conditions often were violated and served as a curtain raiser to deadly guerrilla war, marked by zapping, or ambush attacks on individual gang members or small groups. It was not unusual when a gang was losing a set battle for members to break out switchblades, revolvers, or other forbidden weapons, with the inevitable response from the other side.

The test of champions was, as the name indicates, a battle of two gladiators—usually the presidents, as they were called, of each gang. This was a duel to the finish with specified weapons at a specified place. It was called a "fair one" and the gangs lined up to ensure its "fairness"—a condition which often deteriorated in the violence of passions so that the "fair one" might wind up as a war of extinction.

These conflicts took as many turns as the wars of nations. Some gangs waxed mighty and prideful, extending their turf at the expense of neighbors and establishing a kind of Pax Cobriana over a considerable expanse. Some through alliances and "brother clubs" contended that they held sway over whole areas of the city. Others, badly led, often by suicidal presidents, went into battle after battle until they were wiped off the map.

The gangs were highly structured. Each was led by a president who held virtually dictatorial powers. He was the commander in chief. Nominally elected, he often won his post by a coup d'état against his predecessor. He held office much as did the ancient Scottish chieftains by his wisdom, his cunning, and his courage. "Heart"—as bravery was called—was the preeminent virtue of the bopping gangsters. If a boy had heart—anything would be forgiven him. Heart was not simple bravery. It was élan. It was willingness to "go down" with the odds 10 to 1 against you; it was willingness to "sound" a cop to his face and steal his gun from behind.

Next in command was the vice-president or chief of staff,

who assumed leadership if the president was killed, wounded, or arrested. Each gang had a war minister or minister of defense as well as many "tongues" or scouts, sometimes an armorer (in charge of weapons procurement), and other designated officials. The titles were invariably imposing.

The manner in which the fighting gang, its life-style, its philosophy, its structure, and even its formalities, titles, and division of functions, mimicked the world of nations was so obvious that everyone who came to study it was struck by the parallel. Indeed, it was this which caused many social workers to leap to the easy conclusion that the bopping gangs actually were a product of the divided world, that they caricatured the hostility of the "real" world, that adult bloodshed and national conflicts produced a miniaturized version of the 100 years' war on the streets of New York.

I think the social workers and the newspaper editorialists, the guilt-haunted middle-class theorists, got it all wrong. It seems to me that rather than reflecting the world of the Great Powers (about which Blood and his companions were absolutely and totally ignorant—they could not have told you who Stalin was or what Communism was all about if their lives had depended on it), they constituted, instead, a laboratory example of the behavior of the human animal in stress conditions. The street gangs seem to me to mirror not John Foster Dulles and Vyacheslav Molotov but the early primitive human beings who formed themselves into tribes and extended families to defend themselves against the dark dangers that lurked over the mountain ridge or beyond the nearby river. The principle of territoriality was one of the oldest in the animal world of which we human beings form a singularly important division. So was the principle of the herd or the clan. The distinguishing names of the gangs (as well as distinguishing marks of clothing and conduct) had precedents deep in human history.

The fighting gangs, to my view, were not responding to the

stimuli of the Cold War, they were responding to the stimuli of clear and present danger: to the kid with the switchblade in the street, to the ambush of the gang in the next block, to the prowl car and the random assaults of the police, to the lack of home or family—that is, of any basis of security, to the perceived perils which filled their world. The gang was a microcosm all right. It seemed to me not a laboratory specimen of antisocial young people, as the sociologists of that period tended to assume, but a control group for studying the "real" world, to examine how human beings react by instinct to protect themselves. It seemed to me that on the streets of Red Hook one could easily see the kind of conduct, the interaction and reaction which had marked human relations since the emergence of primitive man. Red Hook was not the exception to the human rule. The exception was our own, cool, comfortable middle class with its built-in apparatus of security (money, position, status, police, government, army). The secure middle class was suspended between two fields of insecurity—the anxiety-filled world of those who like the bopping gangs depended for protection on their own group efforts and (at the other extreme) the anxiety-filled existence of the Great Powers whose security rested on a similar fragile basis.

Surely, the source of violence on the streets was not the blood-and-thunder TV which the moralists excoriated any more than dime novels had provoked the forays of Billy the Kid, the James boys, or the violence of Hell's Kitchen.

Every aspect of the ritualized combat of the bopping gang found its counterpart in primitive social systems—the perception of the stranger as enemy (what youngster has not found himself in this role?), the use of recognition symbols, the concept of the blood brotherhood, the war council—drinking and talking up hatred before "going down" on the other gang (a duplicate of the American Indian war council or the African tribal war dance), the emphasis on shared secrets, the fantasization of "plots" and of grandiose schemes for the defeat of the enemy, the aggrandizement of the enemy, the exaggeration of his hatred and aspirations (the greater the enemy the greater the glory in over-powering him).

What the Shook-Up Generation provided was not, in reality, a picture of "adolescent delinquency" but a portrait of human society as it exists and has existed since the earliest evolutionary times. This society exaggerates many traits which relate to the search for security now so much more sophisticated that many of us fail to recognize the direct mechanisms of social self-protection as they have been transmitted, generation after gen-eration, from the early groupings of animal men who sought to preserve themselves in an intensely hostile and dangerous en-vironment.

Today, not a few of us, bewildered by the world around, feeling our security conceptions jeopardized, seek to find the roots of the danger in adolescent patterns. We try to correlate the adolescent violence of a decade ago with the revolutionary upsurge of today. This is to apply the analogy backwards. The Shook-Up Generation did not threaten the adult world—at least not consciously. Instead, it was trying to create a small island of personal security in an adult world which it found totally threat-ening. Finding no nook or cranny of safety in the slum or street, the youngsters created their own security system, utilizing tradi-tional patterns of conduct.

There is nothing unusual about that. Almost all young people at one time or another feel threatened in the adult world and create neighborhood gangs, fraternities, clubs, passwords, recognition systems, dress symbols, to set themselves apart and give one another an extra-familiar dimension of security.

The same tendencies are carried on into adult life and this explains (in part) the eternal appeal of the secret society, the handclasp, the private key club, the KKK, the night riders, the Birch Society, the Elks, the Knights of Columbus, Phi Beta Kappa, the Union League Club, and even the Playboy Clubs.

I reject the easy and convenient linkage which seeks to establish a common source for the street violence of the bopping gangs and the antisocial conduct of the Shook-Up Generation and the youth movement of today, marked by across-the-board rejection of adult mores and frequently by violent conflict with authority and its symbols.

There *was* violence on the streets in the bopping era, true. But it did not spring from ethical or principled views of the street youths. These were young people with no ideological framework, few socialized relationships, imperfect or nonexistent families, random housing, vague means of support, and characteristically unsympathetic and nonunderstanding relationships with all adults.

They banded together, as they saw it, for protection against a hostile world and fought back against what they perceived as enemies. If there is a parallel between their atavism and any other group, I would say it relates not too distantly to the instinctive reaction of a poorly articulated adult neighborhood or small community against a supposed or vaguely perceived threat.

Perhaps the most stable relationship of the bopping gangs was their ceaseless classic conflict with the police. More about this antagonism in the next chapter.

CHAPTER 7

The Panthers,
the Young Lords,
and the Bishops

Contrary to what some may suppose, the Black Panthers did not suddenly spring forth in U.S. cities as a radical revolutionary agency. They did not arise, *sui generis,* in the slums of Oakland or come to maturity at a cocktail party given by Leonard Bernstein. They are not an invention of the "international Communist conspiracy," especially created to justify J. Edgar Hoover's chronic nightmares. Like it or not, the roots of the Panthers lie deep and tangled in the American tradition.

Ten years ago on the streets of New York the bopping gangs were at their height. They had not yet been fatally weakened by the pervasive spread of heroin. The Mafia had not yet wrought the social work miracle of substituting the nirvana of drug addiction for the deadly terror of the bop. Every neighborhood of the city, a decade ago (with insignificant exceptions—Park Avenue, Midtown, Wall Street) had its teenage fighting gangs. In all there were several hundred active bopping gangs on the register of the Police and the Youth Board.

Two major groups of gangs, the Chaplains and the Bishops, were to be found all over the metropolitan area and even (it was rumored) in other cities. There were supposed to be several score of these affiliated gangs in the city.

Out of this situation arose a simple and exciting fantasy. Some day the Bishops and the Chaplins would come together and set up a joint strategy and planning board. They would devise plans to "take over the city" and on a B (for bopping) Day they would "go down" everywhere. The police would be overwhelmed and the gangs would seize City Hall.

I never heard the fantasy carried beyond that point. To anyone who had seen the pitiful inability of the gang youths to carry out even the simplest plan the unreality of such talk was self-evident. Not only were they incapable of keeping a date within an hour or two of the fixed time but they could not even be certain what day of the week it was. Many had never in their life been more than three or four blocks away from their neighborhood. Some were so illiterate they were terrified of riding on the subway, unable to read the station stop signs, fearful that if they once got into the underground they would never get out. To suppose that youngsters like this could plan and carry out a coordinated operation involving hundreds of units and thousands of individuals was pure moonshine.

Yet, you heard this fantasy discussed gravely and seriously by officials of the Police Department and senior staff members of the Youth Board, which was concerned with keeping down gang violence through its network of "street club workers," social

workers who actually worked in the streets, attaching themselves
to the various teenage gangs. I cannot say that they entirely believed in the possibility of citywide gang war, but they talked as
though they did, sitting around over coffee after midnight and a
long day and evening of trying to cool two belligerent gangs.
There were police officers who took the notion of a citywide uprising quite seriously, seriously enough to engage in contingency
coordination, establishment of liaison between different areas of
the city, preparation of counterinsurgency schemes.

Not infrequently I listened to members of the fighting gangs
talk about the prospects of a citywide rumble. One gang leader
was very proud of his affiliation with the Chaplains and the fact
that there were Chaplains in every part of the city. The day
would come, he was confident, when the Chaplains would suddenly strike a simultaneous blow from the Bronx to East Harlem,
from Bedford-Stuyvesant to the lower East Side. That would be
the day.

Sometimes, it seemed as though the target of this fantasy
would be all the other rival gangs. Sometimes, it would seem that
the target would be the city itself. And sometimes, it was quite
clear, the primary objective would be the police.

For alongside the deadly war which the gangs waged against
one another (incidentally, of course, inflicting no little damage
upon schools, housing projects, commercial establishments, and,
indeed, almost everything with which they came in contact),
there was another basic conflict which went on day and night,
one which embraced not only bopping gang members but almost
all the youth of the slums (and a good portion of the adults). This
was the battle with the police. Conflict with the police was the
fundamental condition of life in Bedford-Stuyvesant or Red Hook.
Every boy in the neighborhood knew that if he was walking down
the street and a prowl car appeared, the occupants of the car
were likely to storm out, beat him up, and possibly run him in.

The bopping gangs hated the police. They were the natural enemy. The police were one reason for the existence of the gang. Together the members felt some security against police attack (although they knew very well that the mere existence of the gang was more apt than not to provoke intensified if random police violence). Red Hook did not have to wait for the Chicago convention to witness a police riot. Red Hook grew up in the tradition of indiscriminate daily police beatings. Squad cars prowled Bedford every evening. If a bunch of youngsters was spotted on the corner, the patrolmen were out of their cars in a twinkling, nightsticks flying, cracking heads and bony shoulders as fast as their arms could rise and fall. The nightstick symbolized law and order in Red Hook and it was no accident that the most spectacular way a gang boy could demonstrate "heart" was by stealing a policeman's nightstick, preferably wrenching it out of his hand.

The police resented and opposed the Youth Board's efforts on the streets. This was called "mollycoddling." It was applying "social work" psychology to a "police problem." The plain fact was that it introduced a variable into a traditional enmity. The police did not want anyone interfering with the age-old street relationship and they strongly suspected that the Youth workers sympathized with the street youth and that the Youth workers might learn too much about the way in which the law of the nightstick was administered. They made their attitude evident in dozens of ways, including beating up and throwing Youth workers themselves into jail.

The assumption of hostility was so high on both sides that the principal problem of the Youth workers was to demonstrate to the street youth that they were not, in fact, spies, provocateurs, or undercover agents of the police. The street youth attitude was that only the police had ever shown an interest in them; therefore the Youth workers must, in some fashion, be playing the police game.

The law of the nightstick was so deeply ingrained that the street youth simply envied the police. As they saw it, the cops had it made. They could walk down the street, slug anyone they wanted, even shoot them, take what they wanted from the stores, collect their cut from the numbers man, beat up the kids, lay the whore for free. There was nothing they couldn't get away with because they were the law. The street youth envied the policeman's status. They hoped, many of them, to be policemen. Or if not policemen then members of an adult criminal gang. That was almost as good.

Most of the policemen had come up from the streets. They understood the street psychology. They were not bothered by it. They often talked about their own days as kids. Sure, the cop on the beat had let them feel the end of his nightstick when they had gone too far. Nothing wrong with that. It had helped them to grow up. What bothered them about contemporary youth was that it seemed, so they said, to be more vicious than they had been. The gangs were better organized, for one thing. They fought with different weapons—switchblades, car aerials, zip guns, bicycle chains, even beretas and other kinds of guns. In the policeman's youth, as he remembered it, the weapons were less lethal—bricks and stones and maybe an occasional beer bottle. But nobody was ever killed. This, of course, was a romanticization. One day I had a talk with Police Commissioner Stephen Kennedy. After contrasting the violence of contemporary street youth with the streets in which he grew up, he recalled how the boys in Red Hook used to get up on the tenement roofs and push garbage cans filled with ashes or bricks down on the police on the pavement, killing and injuring several in this hardly romantic kind of street sport.

I do not want to suggest that the slum youths regarded the roles of the policeman and the adult gangster as interchangeable.

That is unfair. But it is true that the street youth aspired to either of these roles. More often than not the adult policeman and the adult gang member grew up in the same block, attended the same schools, and fought side-by-side on the streets of Red Hook or Chelsea.

I think that an understanding of the street gangs and the gang-police relationship helps to put the roles of the Young Lords, the Blackstone Rangers, and the Black Panthers into a more realistic context than is usually perceived.

I am not suggesting that the Lords, the Rangers, and the Panthers are the same thing. Nor that they are the same as the Chaplains and the Bishops. But all share certain traits of origin and conduct. This may easily be seen in the case of the Blackstone Rangers, a brother gang from Chicago's South Side, organized in almost the same manner as the Chaplains or the Bishops, dedicated to almost the same kind of security interests, indulging in the same range of activities in the south Chicago slums, impacted in the same traditionally hostile way vis-à-vis the Chicago police and then, gradually moved, in much the same manner that some of the fighting gangs in New York neighborhoods were ten years ago, a certain distance away from basically antisocial and destructive habits into patterns which became increasingly social and political.

It made this transition but it did not lose all its characteristics as a typical street gang. Nor did the police abandon their traditional hostility to it as a street gang. Instead their hostility and suspicion was intensified by the new sociopolitical image of the Rangers. The cops did not buy that. Once a Ranger (i.e., a street youth) always a Ranger ("A Bishop is always a Bishop"). The way to cope with a Ranger was with the nightstick. If the Rangers were trying to give themselves the air of being noncriminal and nonviolent—so much more the reason for police hostility and suspicion. At best it was a put-on. At worst it might and probably did challenge the rule of the nightstick.

Now, without going into specific details (and the conflict in the Chicago streets has taken a more and more deadly turn) the typical Ranger did not suddenly become a button-down-collar Eugene McCarthy type. He remained what he had been—a street youth with all the uncertainties, anxieties, paranoia, antagonisms, economic binds, and, quite possibly, addictions to narcotics or tendencies toward petty crime which he had before. What had happened was that he was, more or less successfully, trying to channel his frustrations, his resentments, his aggressions, into socially motivated purposes. But he had not undergone an overnight transformation. He was still an uncertain, erratic problem youth—inconsistent, often unreliable, socially active today and socially destructive tomorrow. No one who has met or worked with youth from the streets has any illusion as to the enormous problems each struggles with. He has been subjected to almost every damaging, degrading, and dangerous influence which society possesses. He is young, untrained, unskilled, undisciplined, and often unstable. With the best of intentions and the best of opportunities his performance will be erratic. This should surprise no one. One night he will turn up at a meeting dedicated to black power, to a radical program for transforming the condition of Chicago's South Side. The next he may be involved once again in the kind of adolescent violence which was the hallmark of the bopping gang ten years ago. A few nights later the scene may center on marijuana or even hard drugs. Stability, reliability, consistency are qualities which mature adults find difficulty in achieving. Small wonder that they are not readily within the grasp of the teenage street youth.

What is true of the Rangers is true in some measure of the Panthers. The origin of the Panthers is to be found in the same street youth, the same street gangs, the same mores, the same problems, the same groping efforts at security within the concept of the street group. It is no accident that the Panther organization uses titles drawn straight from the context of the decade-old bopping gangs—the minister of information, the minister of defense, etc. It is no accident that the watchword of the Panthers is Defense—the use of weapons and force to protect its membership against assault from without. This comes direct from the lexicon of the bopping gang. The Bishop or the Chaplain belonged to his gang as a measure of self-defense, of protection. It began precisely the same with the Panthers. Their psychology derives directly from this basic concept. Do the Panthers engage in aggressive acts? I do not know. But I know that the street gang engages in aggression under the slogan of defense. The preclusive attack is no monopoly of police or of European statesmen. The street gang shouting the slogan of defense will carry out an assault on a hostile or enemy gang in order, as they explain, to forestall a similar attack by the hostile group on themselves.

Nothing has been more characteristic of the brief and violent life of the Panthers than the deadly combat in which they find themselves engaged with the police. In city after city and occasion after occasion there has been a shoot-out or fatal encounter of one sort or another. Uniformly the Panthers blame the police for the violent attacks. They contend that the police are engaged in a national drive of extermination, a deliberate campaign in which they assert (with more than a few examples of evidence) that the FBI has lent a hand to wipe them off the earth.

One need not accept the entire scenario as projected by the Panthers to observe that the fatal toll of Panther killings has risen to very high levels. Something has caused a large number of Panthers to die under the guns of the police. Something has brought an unusual number of the survivors into prisons and courtrooms convicted or charged with extremely serious crimes. And now something is causing an increasing number of police to die in sniper attacks in the ghettos.

If the deadly combat between the Panthers and the police is placed within the framework of the traditional rule of the streets by nightstick, the traditional use of force by the police to cow and repress aggressive (and nonaggressive) youth in the streets, a good many of its facets become clearer.

In the case of the Panthers there is not only the question of self-defense; there are their ostentatious warnings of gun-carrying, of the use of weapons for self-protection. There is the deliberate employment of ferocious rhetoric against the police—a characteristic extension of another street custom—"sounding." Sounding is not necessarily unknown in the white middle-class world. But it is a common everyday phenomenon on the black street. In it the street youths (and adults) vie in improvisation and imaginative insult and rhetoric. Sounding finds its greatest virtuosos among blacks. Because it is not part of Puerto Rican culture or ethic, it has again and again been the cause of fatal encounters or suicides among Puerto Rican youths to whom the mother oath can be avenged only with the life of the perpetrator. Sounding is almost routinely characteristic of the Panthers and of their characteristics none arouses more deep resentment (or bewilderment) than this incandescent rhetoric, this iteration and reiteration of mother oaths, this oratorical kill and overkill. But no one familiar with sounding and the encounters in which street youths vie and vie against one another for new heights of insult can fail to recognize the origin of this nerve-racking custom (which has now been enthusiastically co-opted by white radical youth).

It would certainly be a mistake to characterize the Panthers as super-Bishops, some kind of 3-D Chaplains, some kind of politicized street gang. They carry today far too great political and social content, have come too far in establishing themselves as an action group which acts out on the national stage the suppressed hatred and frustrations of their black brothers who almost universally sympathize with them.

Nor should it be supposed that street gangs are incapable of major political impact. We have not known them in a large-scale way in the United States since the middle of the last century. But, of course, they are a familiar phenomenon in Asian and Middle Eastern countries. Street gangs are drawn into the political arena by rising social conflict when their own leaders (and political forces outside the streets) move to harness their energy, force and violence to programmatic or charismatic causes. They have been a political factor in Japan for decades. It is a measure of our political naïveté that the only comparison which has found its way into our common usage is the comparison with the Nazi street bullies. Street action was no monopoly of the Nazis. It just happens to be a spectacular form with which Americans are more familiar than some of the others.

The fascists possess no monopoly of organized street violence. Street gangs have played a much more prominent part in revolutions than is usually recognized (or admitted) once they are over. We remember the Budapest uprising of 1956 with emotion and admiration—the brave Budapest youths fighting bare-handed against Russian tanks. The image is accurate but I know from interviewing scores of Hungarian refugees who fled to the U.S.A. that it was not only the poets and patriotic democrats who fought in the Budapest streets against the Russians. The street gangs of the city, apolitical slum youth, turned out en masse and fought with the kind of "heart" that would have won instant recognition in Red Hook or Bedford-Stuyvesant.

Violence attracts the violent whether it is political or narrowly antisocial. Anyone who knows the life of the streets, who has watched the police maintain the rule of the nightstick through generation after generation, cannot fail to perceive the critical characteristics which render the Panther-Police combat no strange and inexplicable phenomenon but something which, to paraphrase the famous words of Stokeley Carmichael, is as American as cherry pie. Ten years ago policemen dreamed that the Chaplains might rise and take over the city. Today they dream that the Panthers may rise and take over the country.

Neither vision possesses a logical basis. Both contain a kind of adolescent yearning for Armageddon. And both, to be certain, overlook completely the mundane and practical matter of logistics and coordination.

CHAPTER 8

Where Have All the Flowers Gone?

Speaking at a symposium of critics of *The New York Times* which marked the end of the decade of the '60s, Hilton Kramer observed that the great Woodstock, New York, youth festival of summer, 1969, stood as a watershed in American mood and culture. "It'll never be as peaceful again," he said.

I think he is right. In a sense, within a year Woodstock had become obsolete, a nostalgic dream, a utopian ideal, a moment when time stood still, or possibly an event which never happened, was just imagined by 300,000 people who dreamed the same dream and then awakened to the same ugly, continuing, worsening reality.

I did not go to Woodstock. I wish I had. It was, I suppose, the Lourdes of our day or, in another sense, without the danger and the disease, the Children's Crusade of our time. It was a crusade by the pure of heart in the company of the multitude of pure of heart, of the deep-flowing, open, out-going and out-giving strain in our youth—a strain which is, to be sure, childish, which may be out of touch with the "serious" concerns of the elders and almost deaf to the existence of those concerns. Yet, it is a strain which is impeccably attuned to great moral issues, the issues of life and death, both in Asia and in America, of freedom and repression, of generosity and selfishness, of honesty and hypocrisy.

In Russia in the old days (and the tradition persists into the present more than you might imagine) there were persons called "God's fools" who walked about the country, plain people, sometimes quite simpleminded, sometimes clearly idiots. They wandered over the countryside in bast shoes and rough, brown kaftans, endlessly making pilgrimages and endlessly dependent on the piety and generosity of the peasants for a plate of milk and kasha, a barn to sleep in in summer, a place on the tile stove in winter. They were, by and large, kept safe from harm by their trust in the people, and it was a trust which was not often betrayed, for the tradition of common charity ran (and runs) deep in Russia, the tradition of sharing, particularly if there is little to share, with those who have nothing at all—persons like "God's fools," or étape convicts, escaped prisoners, or others who in the general and continuous state of Russian oppression are deemed inexorably to have a call upon the more fortunate.

Those who went to Woodstock were not God's fools. But there was in them a strain of that simple faith, that unworldliness, that unbroken confidence that man is good, that his trust will not be betrayed.

It was this characteristic which flowed out of the Woodstock Nation, which welled out of the scores of thousands of personal relationships, and which was, to the surprise of the whole country, perceived by all, felt by all. No one, I am certain, who was part of Woodstock will ever lose what it gave him. And for those of us who shared the experience vicariously the glow will long be alive.

By the same token I think Kramer was right. I do not think there will be another Woodstock. In fact, each effort to recreate Woodstock either on large or small scale in the ensuing months produced disaster mounting to the deadly Hell's Angels episode in which a man was murdered in full sight of thousands and others were brutally beaten at the December, 1969, convocation of the Rolling Stones at Altamont Speedway in California. It was six months by the calendar from Woodstock to Altamont. But in real time they were light-years apart.

Woodstock was every boy and girl's dream of Walking Through the Looking Glass, of The Other Side of the North Wind, of The Emerald City of Oz. In fact, Woodstock *was* the Emerald City of Oz-updated, updated with rock and pot and peace. Woodstock was Woodstock, in part, because of sheer numbers. Everyone looked about and for as far as he could see there was no one to be seen except himself, an endless reflection of self-images in every direction. It was stirring, overpowering, so overpowering that it wrought its own remarkable effect not only on the countryside and the country people into whose midst Woodstock poured but on the whole country, which caught the Woodstock contagion, surprisingly and almost in spite of itself.

But it was a light fever and it passed quickly, leaving only a faint rash on the national consciousness. A year later people who had not been to Woodstock rubbed their eyes a bit and wondered how it could have happened and what was real about it. And people who had been at Woodstock, looking back at it across the new barriers, the Panther murders, the Tate murders, the Cambodian murders, the Augusta murders, the Kent State murders, the Jackson murders, the Agnew rhetoric, rubbed their eyes, too. Could it really have happened?

It did happen. But as Kramer said, it will not happen again. It will never be so peaceful again. Because Woodstock is an unsupportable idealization, an island of sweetness in a sea of acid, a mass philosophical cop-out. The path to Woodstock leads to

Woodstock. It goes no further and once the island of Woodstock has been achieved it begins to shrink until finally there is no island, there is no Woodstock, there is only the memory of the dream and the reality of Altamont.

In December, 1969, John Lennon and Yoko Ono paid, I suppose, $20,000 or it could have been $30,000 to put a block-long advertising sign up in Times Square. It said "Peace Now . . . If You Want It." What did it mean? It meant what Woodstock meant—that if everyone who wanted peace simply walked away from war (that is, walked off the war jobs, the war-connected jobs, paid no war taxes, heeded no war calls, declared themselves *out* of the war, here, now, and completely)—the war was over. Well, I suppose that was true or could have been true, although the ability of the Pentagon machine to keep on running even with a few million missing parts is probably greater than John Lennon and Yoko Ono realized.

But, like Woodstock, this meant walking out of the real world, the square world, into the world of disconnection; it meant drop-out on a scale of millions and not just as at Woodstock for a weekend, or maybe, as it was for some, for a summer. It meant drop-out, period. Drop-out in numbers that would bring the whole grinding terrifying machine of the modern military state to a halt. The war would end.

And this, alas, on practical terms, was not going to happen. Not that thousands and tens of thousands were not dropping out. They were. Some to the beaches of California and Oregon. Some to the byways of the earth, the real byways—Istanbul, Peshawar, Kabul, Vientiane, Nepal—to live the lives of mendicant hashish heads. Some to homesteads in South Dakota or Saskatchewan. Some to the East Village or the dregs of Haight-Ashbury. And many many more to the commune or the group, the extended family or the tribe. Some, into tribes as bizarre and deadly as that headed by Charles Manson. But most of them in the same kind of purity, idealism, moral disassociation from the evils of the straight world which gave nineteenth-century America Harmony, Indiana; Chautauqua, New York; or the Brook Farm experiment—clusters of men and women, usually but not always young, bound, in part, by revulsion from the materialism and object-fetish of the American way and, in part, by the dream of a new and finer relationship of men and women, seeking to create their own world within the confines of the old, seeking to put at a distance the money-grubbing, hypercompetitive, achievement-oriented, homogenized existence in which they were bred and raised for the sake of a new society in which honesty replaced hypocrisy, simplicity complexity, the hand the machine, the heart the brain, candles electricity, the foot the car. Into this mixture has been stirred at times and places a certain measure of hedonism.

To be sure. Some lived on pot and others on wine. Some chopped their wood in the Vermont forest. Others panhandled lower Fifth Avenue. Some lived in cabins and grew their own potatoes and grass. Others inhabited crash pads and endured lice and gonorrhea.

Some were more philosophical than others. Some had money. Some lived on mutual charity. But all were bound by one basic rule—the rule of creating for themselves a world in the image of their own dream. That world did not exist. OK. That world could not be attained for all. OK. So we will make our own world.

This is a deep human obsession. I have seen it in many places. I saw it in the wilds of the Northwest Angle on the Minnesota-Manitoba frontier forty years ago. I've seen it in the Sierras and met the grizzled remnants of the mountain men, living on their own in monastic isolation. I have seen it in the *prigorodny raioni*, the suburbs of Moscow in the blackest Stalin days, the quiet Russians, heads down, living in a little cabin or shack, trusting no one but the closest, most intimate members of their own family, living in a world their own.

Oh, the impulse to make one's own world, to erect a wall against the alien majority must be as old as humanity. It brought the Pilgrims and the Puritans to America and it sent Roger Williams into the wilderness of Connecticut. For a hundred years Americans hitched their oxen or horses to a wagon and headed west on the same illusory mission, welding the dream of creating their own world to the dream of the pot of gold at the end of the rainbow.

And, of course, the parallel direct and clear can be found in the idealistic colonies that spattered the wilderness of America more than 100 years ago—the utopian colonists with their egalitarianism, their unworldliness (no money, no ownership), their insistence on self-sufficiency (no matter if it meant linsey-woolsey and pine-stick candles and homespun britches), their new moral systems, their transcendentalism, their rights-for-women, their free love, their polygamy or polyandry, their new revelations, their vision of man's perfectability, their certainty that utopia was achievable against all reason, against all logic.

Indeed, you can match the principles of almost any American commune of the nineteenth century against those of the twentieth. The differences are subliminal. In practice and in belief they are part and parcel of the same human current.

Now, I don't mean to equate rock music, hash, and crash pads with the frosty philosophy of Wendell Phillips. But examine the arguments, the questions which Brook Farm debated until its inevitable collapse. They are the same issues that harass the idealists of today. The line from Brook Farm to Woodstock could not run more straight and true.

There is a difference. Woodstock was mass. Brook Farm was, if you'll pardon the expression, class. More realistically we are dealing with two aspects of the same phenomenon. Woodstock was an outpouring of individuals in search of their own dream. Brook Farm or the contemporary Vermont commune is an effort to create that dream, objectively, in the midst of and in spite of a hostile society. There were, of course, mass equivalents of Woodstock in the last century—the "encampments," the great spiritual and moral crusades.

And there was the same clash between activism and withdrawal, between Julia Ward Howe, Harriet Beecher Stowe, John Brown—the radical abolitionists (the moral equivalent of, shall we say, the Peace Coalitions, the SDS, and the Weathermen), and those who, despairing of getting their fellow men to turn away from perceived evils, themselves turned their backs on the world and set about the construction of a citadel of the spirit.

So, we can establish with ease and virtuosity the credentials and lineage of Woodstock. Unfortunately, at the same time we can, as Hilton Kramer so acutely noted, forecast its doom. The doom may not be Altamont and Hell's Angels. It may not be (as many have warned, and feared, and some have devotedly hoped for and planned for) a bloody confrontation in the streets of Washington with machine gunners and tanks offering a 1970s rerun of General MacArthur's white horse charge that drove thousands of Bonus Marchers in 1932 from the Capitol environs. But doomed it is. Doomed because the walls of the materialist fortress will not come tumbling down at the sounding of a pure high note. The masses will not put their fate and their life-style into the hands of the meek, the humble, the barefoot, the bearded, the braless. The mass crusade, Woodstock, Reflecting Pool splash-ins, surging throngs of the committed and the nonsquare do move the country. But not that much. This is the lesson the blacks have found, time and again. The march to Selma, the march on Washington, the tired and weary ploddings from one end of the South to another, the great rallies, the huge meetings, the masses on the steps of capitals and in city squares—these do move the country. But only inch-by-inch and foot-by-foot, and the struggle must go on and on, time without end, winning and rewinning the same simple points. It is like a struggle with the tide. It can be won but only a little at a time, only with great endurance, and it can be kept won only with eternal vigilance. Woodstock is not patience, endurance, vigilance, militance. Woodstock is love.

There are those who, perhaps, will resent the comparison. I see Woodstock in the spirit of the Sermon of the Mount and, alas, it took not Matthew but the militant Paul to forge the cohesive fighting body of believers which was able, in the end, to overcome the Praetorians of Rome and the fanatic counter-faiths which surrounded the young Christians.

Woodstock is in the tradition of Thoreau and Rousseau. It is Walden Pond and the *Noble Sauvage* set to music by the Beatles. But it does not lead to the new Jerusalem. It cannot. I am sorrier than I can say that this cannot be, because the image of the flower people, the image of giving of oneself without asking, of asking without thinking, of sharing without waiting, is the golden rule for which generations of human beings have striven, or so they have thought and felt. It is the Christian ethic. It is Buddha's teaching. It is what Karl Marx for all his muddled Teutonic economics was all about. It is, if I read him right (and no one can be sure of this), what Mao Tse-tung hopes to leave as a legacy to his people. It is the perfection of man—here and now. In Woodstock Nation. And it will not, it cannot, it will not be permitted to occur.

I am not going on these pages to attempt to prove the un-perfectability of man. I happen to believe man can be perfected, after a fashion. But I cite one testimony in evidence of the diffi-culty of perfecting him. This is the historical fact that man never has been perfected. Not in any numbers. Not in Greece or Rome; not in ancient China or modern Russia. Not in India or Egypt. Not in the catacombs of the martyrs. Certainly not in the United States.

Each of these societies has striven in its own way for a more perfect order. Some have tried with faith. Others with cynical skill. But one one has come close. Neither Rousseau's *Noble Sauvage* or Piers Plowman, not Jefferson's dream or Christ's vision, not Plato, not Lenin. It has not happened yet, although a thousand times man has cried as Lincoln Steffens did on his first view of Soviet Russia, "I've seen the Future—and it works!" Would that Steffens had been right! As one who has watched the "new Soviet man," has seen how faithfully he incarnates the Old Russian, how assiduously he emulates the most tawdry materialism of the hated capitalist West, how short he falls from the Communist dream of man without greed, without envy, without fear, without hate, dedicated to the good and the noble, I know how the odds have been stacked against Woodstock. Woodstock, lovely Woodstock, is fated to live on in Altamont. It was born to preside over its own sadistic death. Its only life is the gossamer veil it has spun in our minds as the vision that might have been, its only hope that the legend of its being will inspire future generations to strive in some new world for its fulfillment.

CHAPTER 9

Highs and Lows

When I was a youngster in Minneapolis I knew a boy at West Side High who drank a bottle of gin (probably a fifth of bootleg Gordon's) without stopping for breath. Someone dared him to drink it as he stood outside of Hazen's Drugstore one long, summer evening. He tilted his head back, upended the bottle, and let it pour down his throat. He staggered a bit, tried to speak, and fell to the sidewalk. By the time they got him to the hospital he was dead.

In my college days the university paper was printed at the *Tidende,* a Norwegian daily newspaper. The printers at the *Tidende,* cut off from their supply of schnapps by Prohibition, substituted pure grain alcohol. To work with them you had to drink with them. They gave you an option. You could have hot or cold water for a chaser after throwing down half a water glass of 188-proof hospital alcohol (I imagine it had been cut considerably, but 188 proof was what we supposed it to be). It did not kill you but it paralyzed you from head to toe. One of the *Tidende* printers made a mistake one night. He downed a 10-ounce bottle of wood alcohol before he knew what he was drinking. They saved his life but he lost his sight.

The rule on drinking in those days, and it held for every youngster I knew, was, Drink whatever there is. There may not be any more.

Some of us used to drive across the border from Minnesota into Ontario during vacation time. Liquor was licensed in Ontario. You registered in a hotel, went to the state liquor store, bought your permit, and purchased your limit of booze—I think you could buy two quarts of whiskey a day. Within an hour of arriving in Port Arthur we would be dead drunk in the hotel. That was the purpose of drinking. To get as drunk as you could as quick as you could.

Today the prohibition movement seems like something dreamed up for the musical comedy stage. But it wasn't funny. Nor did it come into being because of eccentricity or the flamboyant character of Carry Nation and crusaders like her. Prohibition came into being because millions of Americans were drinking themselves blind in saloons. They always had. Read any of the reports of travelers to the U.S.A. in the nineteenth century, early or late. Americans swilled liquor on a scale which makes even present-day Siberia seem mild. Nor, to be honest, was the situation much different in other countries. England and Scotland, for example. And, notably, the Scandinavian countries.

Drink was a social, economic, and moral problem of the first magnitude—quite likely the first problem of the day. It had been so before the Industrial Revolution and it became even more so with the Revolution and the huge displacement of populations from peasant cottages to factory barracks. It was the harridan-handmaiden of the millions who swarmed to American shores throughout the nineteenth century, to build the railroads, to open up the lands, to man the mines, the factories, to fill the industrial slums. Not the least useful use of whiskey was to addict the Red Indian and render him an easy, sodden mark for the acquisition of his lands.

It seems quaint and naïve to us that when Prohibition ended and liquor was legalized most states forbade the return of the "saloon"; even the use of the word was forbidden, giving rise to the endless proliferation of today's pantywaist euphemisms—bars, grills, lounges, pubs, ad nauseam. This was no accident. The saloon was indelibly imprinted in people's minds as the symbol of all that was the worst about alcohol—the deliberate encouragement of drunkenness, the grim commercialization of alcoholism as a pattern of life, the enslavement and impoverishment of those already enslaved and impoverished, the corruption of human existence to the lowest possible denominator—in the flaunted, open pursuit of profit and greed. The saloons were in large numbers "tied"—that is, owned or controlled by the great breweries and distilleries which remorselessly pressed the saloonkeepers to raise and raise again the averages of consumption. They were the center of the vice and debasement of the urban proletariat, the command posts of criminal political systems, the control mechanism for the entrepreneurs—the great Chicago packing plants, the great Pittsburgh steel mills, the Pennsylvania coal barons, the textile kings of Lawrence and Paterson—to ensure the docility and availability of an endless source of cheap labor. (In pre-Communist Russia Lenin and his Bolsheviks correctly identified the State Vodka Monopoly as the linchpin of the oppression of the proletariat. Little did they guess that with time the Bolshevik Vodka Monopoly would come to serve the same purpose).

Alcohol has accompanied man, I suppose, since he sat around the caves of Lescany lighting fires to keep back the sabertooth tigers. And alcohol has been a factor, at least, in the lives of many other animals who come to browse on the overripe grapes and staggered away, bellies distended and limbs unaccountably unstable.

Prohibition, of course, did not end the relationship of Americans to alcohol. It merely introduced superficially new habit patterns and imposed a grid of incredibly profitable corruption on the existing and evolving relationships of criminals and law-enforcement agencies--police, treasury men, internal revenue men, sheriffs' deputies. Whoever had a badge found that Prohibition made it a much more profitable emblem. (We are still suffering from the symbiotic relationships created by Prohibition—the Big Business-Crime Syndicate-Police Syndrome.)

And people went on drinking, went on addicting themselves to alcohol, particularly the young. Alcohol like nicotine was a traditional part of the puberty ritual, the coming of age, along with the first sex experiences, the first time boys and girls "went all the way." Prohibition did not end addiction to alcohol. All the alcoholics of my generation became addicted under Prohibition. In those days the only difference between adolescent drinking and adult drinking was that the adult, usually, recognized that it would be possible to get another drink and thus did not necessarily throw down every possible kind and variety of drink as fast as he could pour them from the bottle because soon the bottle would be empty and who knew when another would come along.

Naturally, the adult did not regard himself as an addict. Usually, he prided himself on being a "good drinker." He downed his three martinis for lunch, his three martinis before dinner, his four to six Scotches after dinner, plus the quick slug from the bottle before bed, and got used to waking up morning after morning with a headache and hangover which might or might not vanish before the saving glow of the early lunch-hour martinis. He was not certain exactly how much he drank each day but he might calculate it as "about a fifth." Not a bad addiction. (But compare this to the "three-bottle men" of Soames Forsyte's generation—that is, three bottles of Port or Madeira consumed *after* a dinner at which half a dozen wines and liqueurs were served and liberally consumed.)

There has been a great deal of philosophizing about the

effects of Prohibition on American mores. I don't think, on the average, that it made all that difference. Americans young and old drank a great deal before Prohibition. They probably drank a little less during Prohibition because liquor was not quite so readily available and was often more expensive, but perhaps, because of the psychological thrill of the forbidden fruit, they may have enjoyed it more. It is true that Prohibition encouraged a general crumbling of mores, morals, and respect for law. There is nothing like a bad law for infecting the whole statutory barrel, as King George III learned with his infamous efforts to put a tax on tea.

It has been held, and I entirely agree, that the scofflaw attitudes of a major segment of the public toward Prohibition and the Volstead Act brought into being a whole nation with little or no respect for the law. Leaving aside the question of how deep-seated a tradition of law observation and law enforcement the country actually possessed (and the then and now living tradition of vigilantism and "rural justice" makes the proposition at least arguable), there can be no doubt that Prohibition, rumrunning, the bootlegger, the speakeasy, Al Capone, the Syndicate, and the Cop Payoff savagely corrupted the country's legal system. I think it can be demonstrated that a similar situation has been created by the present drug scene. Laws against marijuana are so casually flouted by the majority of the population under the age of twenty-five and by a large percentage of those under thirty-five or forty that the dichotomy of the Prohibition era has been recreated. The parallel can be carried further by matching the organized liquor traffic with its international ramifications and tentacles reaching into every political nook and cranny with the even more elaborate international narcotics trade affiliations in almost every country: links with all means of transportation, extraordinary banking and financing tie-ups, profits of billions of dollars, providing a war chest which readily buys free passage through any law-enforcement barrier that frustrated and honest officials attempt to set up.

If booze corrupted a whole nation in the 1920s, dope is doing the same to the greater part of the world today.

But dope has by no means displaced drink except, perhaps, among certain segments of the "youth market." In the nearly forty years since the end of Prohibition, drinking patterns have changed little. Millions of Americans remain liquor addicts. Of course, they resent the idea, reject it with indignation. They can take a drink or leave it. Fact is they take it, and they take it every day. The dose may be fixed, relatively small in ounces, or it may be huge and incapacitating. But it is regular. Automatic. A remarkable percentage of the American populace is hooked on alcohol as is a remarkable percentage of the world population. Still, you can ask any American if we have a liquor problem and he will think you are making things up.

While I am not trying to start a new crusade against demon rum (although that is not altogether a bad idea), I do want to put into a more reasonable context the so-called drug scene.

Almost all opinions about the drug scene, pro or con, are so heavily laden with emotion that obviously what is involved here is not whether drugs are good or bad, per se (and I happen to think they are bad, across-the-board bad, although some less bad than others), but an assault on life-styles.

Addiction to alcohol we have lived with so long that we recognize it, accept it, expect it, fight it, sometimes, in individual cases, but often do not even perceive that it exists.

Drugs, no. Drugs are to most older adults reared in the European or "Western" tradition a perversion, a vile abomination, a subject of intense fear, of intense hate, blind anger, terror, revulsion—you name it. There is not much difference in the response whether we are talking of marijuana, speed, heroin, hash, or hallucinogens. The fact is that drug usage and drug addiction are seen by many adults as an alien culture, probably Oriental, and certainly depraved. The needle conjures up visions of the Buenos Aires white slave traffic and hidden paperbacks hastily, hectically scanned in schoolhouse toilets or behind the barn. To be sure there may be drug skeletons in the family closet. But these only heighten the terror. Dope = degradation = death.

Well, I am the last person to argue against the deadly danger of dope. Nations have been weakened to the point of collapse by it, the most notable example being China where, although we may not like to recall this, much of the country was deliberately and artificially brought to opium addiction in order to make profits for the British East India Company. It is also a fact that when the transcontinental railroad was being built across the United States and thousands of Chinese coolies were imported to work on the tracks, the fine old pioneer railroad managements laid in liberal stocks of opium and morphine, which they sold in preference to whiskey freely over the counter in the company commissaries that were the only places the Chinese could spend their money. The reason? Higher profit ratios.

It is not just a bad-taste joke perpetrated by Westbrook Pegler that the Roosevelts and many other good New York and Boston families which engaged in the clipper trade to China turned a tidy profit in opium. It is a fact. Perhaps today's Mafia may find an instructive moral in this circumstance. It is undeniable that mass addiction to opium (or any other drug) produces totally disastrous personal and social consequences. The spread of the use of opium and its derivatives throughout Asia had profound social and economic and political repercussions— repercussions which persist to this day.

But I think that it might be argued that Asian addiction was not always and singly a one-way ticket to hell. In some circumstances, in some conditions, it might be the only passage to heaven the diseased, starving, doomed coolie could possess. I was once taught an eloquent lesson by Dr. Gremliza, an eccentric German who dedicated his life to the disease-stricken, poverty-wracked villages of the southern Khuzistan in Persia. Addiction was high—possibly 80 percent—among men and women of these villages where he worked. The life expectancy of these people was twenty-six to twenty-eight years. They were sufferers of congenital syphilis, trachoma, tuberculosis, typhoid, and bilharziasis, every disease of malnutrition, water pollution, and generations of raddled heritage. But, doctor, I exclaimed. Can't anything be done about their addiction (to opium and hash)? Surely, when they have so little money it should be spent for food. He looked at me sadly. Are you sure? he said. Suppose they have a few cents. If they buy food they will still be hungry, their lungs will still be wracked by endless coughing, the dysentery will not halt, the horrible vista of their world will continue to envelop them like a shroud from which there is no escape—and, of course, there is no escape. But if they spend those pennies for opium they are released from the horror of the present, the unchanging, unchangeable horror of the present, and for a little time can float off into dreams where hunger vanishes, disease vanishes. To be sure, they will die faster. But they die so fast anyway. Are you sure that I should deprive them of the only pleasure the torture of their life affords?

This is an argument which is not easy to answer. If you cannot end the excoriating poverty of the Khuzistan (it has been lifted, incidentally, considerably in recent years through the joint efforts of David Lilienthal and the Shah of Persia), if you cannot bring food, health, and housing to the crepuscular masses of Calcutta, if 150 years ago there was no cure for the enslavement of child labor in the black coalpits of Wales, if there is no means by which the Soviet government can provide housing or recreation for the grim-faced miners of the Kolyma gold fields—then, really, can one in all conscience inveigh against dope addiction or alcohol addiction, as one means, artificial and deadly to be sure, for

providing the doomed with a few moments of ease, repose, comfort, or even ecstasy in an otherwise inexorably tragic existence?
Is it really better to condemn men and women to death at the
age of fifteen or sixteen of tuberculosis or fibrulosis or gangrene
or plain starvation, making them fully conscious of every minute
of their suffering, their agony, their inescapable end, or is there
something to be said for morphine or alcohol? I think a case can
be made.

But this is really a digression. Because I do not believe any
case can be made for the necessity of dope or drugs or alcohol in
the conditions of, say, technetronic America, industrialized Soviet
Russia, bourgeois England and Scandinavia, well-to-do France
and Germany, or prosperous Japan. To be sure, pockets of horror
do exist. But the subsidiary conditions for a massive addiction
culture simply are not present. Not physically, at any rate. So
since we do have in the U.S.A. a widely addicted society—to
alcohol, that is—the case must be made in terms of psychology,
habit, acculturation.

And here, I think, we find the cause of the enormous emotional turmoil which the drug culture has caused in the U.S.A.
We are a society which is traditionally, like Western Europe
and most of the world, accustomed to alcohol addiction. This is
the chemical which we habitually employ to change emotional,
environmental, and social values. We drink to relieve depression,
to make ourselves, so we say, lively and gay, to ease our tensions,
to give us nerve or confidence, to celebrate, oh, we have a thousand
different reasons. But basically they all come down to the use
of alcohol to create predictable emotional and personality
changes. (We are, or many of us are, addicted to tobacco but
in somewhat different ways. We may also be addicted to coffee,
to aspirin, to tea, to betel nut, to cocoa leaves, to a very wide
range of chemicals, but I am only going to consider the major
addictions.)

Now, introduced by the young, employed as the central artifact in a whole iconostasis of alien cultural symbols and conventions, come drugs. Not only are drugs new, not only are they recognized (as liquor is not, really) as inherently dangerous, debasing, and debilitating, they are brought in to displace the comfortable, old-fashioned, well-known, traditional alcohol addiction. Drugs are flaunted at our alcohol-oriented society and defended, at least in part, by attacks upon alcohol itself, raising questions (often of guilt) which the alcohol cultists (that is, most middle-aged people) aren't prepared to handle because they simply do not recognize this description as applying to them.

The middle-aged businessman with his multiple martinis and Scotches believes (implicitly) that he is leading a perfectly respectable, conventional, acceptable, "blameless" kind of a life. If he has two or three too many at the Country Club on Saturday night (and if his wife does, too), this comes within the parameters of social behavior set by society as he knows it. The case of his college classmate and one-time law partner, "Wild Eddie" Blake, who drank himself in and out of institutions for twenty years before killing himself and three innocent persons in a head-on collision on the Northern Parkway one night, seems to him a tragedy but a conventional tragedy, the kind which, alas, happens every day.

But to this man the fact that the police have arrested his seventeen-year-old son and two companions in their car on the Long Island Expressway and confiscated half a dozen bags of pot is very nearly the end of the world. He is by no means sure exactly what pot is and he doesn't know what a bag might be. But his son has been arrested for possession of dope and such a thing has never happened in the family before. What makes it worse is that his son seems to think that pot is perfectly OK, that it should be legalized, that it is "not nearly as bad as liquor," and adds, what the father sadly suspects, that "all the kids use it." The father's lecture about the evils of pot, how one thing leads to another, how it is but a short step from pot to heroin, and how LSD endangers the future generations and speed kills (the father, of course, has only the most teetery notion of what all these chemicals may be) falls as flat as a bride's angel food cake.

There is really no point in examining this kind of dialogue. There is no hope for understanding on either side. The boy gives up his father as impossibly square and stupid. The father begins to take a few extra drinks (increasing his alcohol addiction) as he and his friends discuss the utter and total ruin of the young generation, longhairs, the Weathermen, and other symbols of the youth revolt.

Subliminally, I think, both father and son may sense, although they cannot precisely articulate it, the essence of what drug culture is all about.

Each time there is a major turn between so-called generations, the new generation makes potent use of cultural symbols. If, for example, we look at the sharp cultural change which marked the 1890s (largely in England and France), we find, in addition to a range of new sexual attitudes (greater freedom and variety of heterosexual relationships and a sharp increase in public homosexual manifestations, highlighted by the Oscar Wilde affair), changes in addiction patterns. There was in the 1890s extensive experimentation with and use of opium and cocaine and, particularly in France, absinthe (still defined, no doubt accurately, by the dictionary as a "toxic" green liqueur whose "excessive use may cause delirium and idiocy"). The menace of absinthe addiction was regarded as so acute that its manufacture and sale were forbidden in France and Switzerland and importation into the U.S.A. was banned in 1912. The use of the cigarette dates from this period, replacing the cigar and the Turkish

hubble-bubble. Cigarettes were called by the pre-1900 world
an instrument of the devil—"coffin nails" to be precise. The moral
and social objections to cigarettes were equal in intensity to
those directed against pot today and the consequences to the
users were described (as it happened with unusual and unexpected accuracy) as certain to be fatal.

One can wander backward and forward in history, selecting
samples of the same kind of social attitude. The initial introduction of tobacco into Europe, for example, caused as great a moral
flare-up as LSD—probably greater. Coffee was considered a
dangerous aphrodisiac (it still is in Russia). Only rakes and fast
women touched it.

To come down to more recent times, the great social upheaval which began in the U.S.A. just before World War I and
continued in slightly different form into the "flaming twenties"
was marked by similar outbursts. Gin, for example, was introduced as the new addictive alcohol of the Greenwich Village
rebels. It was instantly condemned by "decent society"—not because it was alcohol but because of the connotations which gin
bore—synonymous with the most wretched dregs of alcohol
culture, thought specifically to injure the brain and to be most
dangerous for young women, as it damaged their child-bearing
capacity. It was known to be highly addictive—unlike good
bourbon whiskey. Along with this came cigarette smoking by
women. This, too, was seen as a particular threat to the repro-
ductive system. In other words, the future of the race was being
endangered by the radical customs of the young.

Thus, it seems to me that drug culture, like it or not—and I
dislike and deplore it—is in the mainstream of youth-oriented
social change. It may be more dangerous than opium and absinthe
(or may not); it may be more dangerous than gin and coffin-
nails (or may not). But it must be seen as one facet, albeit an
extremely important one, of broad-scale youth-innovated cultural

change which runs right across the horizon—a phenomenon by no means new, unusual, or unexpected—although invariably perceived by the adults and the old as threatening, terrifying, devastating, and a sign that the new Gomorrah is at hand—if not already arrived.

CHAPTER 10

Hula Hoops
and the Red Guard

About ten years ago on one of my periodic trips to Russia a young Moscow friend asked me in the confidential half-whisper which many Soviets employ for important and possibly subversive communications:

"What do you do in a hula hoop?"

Not having even been inside a hula hoop I found the question hard to answer, but I quickly discovered what was troubling my friend. He was the proud owner of a hula hoop which had been smuggled in from Poland by his girl friend, who put it under her dress to defy customs examination. It was, the young Russians understood, the latest American fad. They gathered from critical articles which had appeared in *Pravda* and *Literaturnaya Gazeta* that Americans used the hoops in some sexy, obscene, or possibly pornographic manner, but exactly what they did inside a hula hoop they had not been able to figure out. The Russian and his girl friend had squeezed themselves inside the hoop but once there they did not know what to do. The hoop was an article of considerable importance to them. The girl had risked possible arrest and certain condemnation by smuggling it in and had paid about $50 for the hoop on the Polish black market. Now they wanted to take full advantage of it, by doing as the Americans did, and, of course, to impress their friends by their advanced and daring behavior. When I told my friend that, to the best of my knowledge, Americans just put the hoop around their waist and wiggled to make it turn around and around he was disappointed. I had the distinct feeling that when he and his girl friend demonstrated the hula hoop at the next party at one of their friends' apartments they were going to offer gyrations considerably more exciting than those I described.

Hula hoops have long since vanished from youth culture not only in the United States but in Poland and even in Russia. The incident has no importance except as evidence of the pervasive spread of customs and styles from one end of the world to another. I have listened to rock music in Ulan Bator and Gangtok. I have played Beatles records on jukeboxes (German-made) in the Persian desert and on Soviet steamers traversing the Sea of Japan. I have studied the texts of decrees in Burma banning long hair and miniskirts; I have read Komsomol speeches delivered in Urals factories, inveighing against long hair and miniskirts; I have seen warnings from the Kuomintang against long hair and miniskirts, and I have seen the same from the Greek colonels. The continents and countries change but not the message.

For years Russian-language programs of the Voice of America had small Soviet audiences because of the intensity of Russian jamming. Now jamming is more apt to be intermittent but the audiences are not much bigger. But the VOA's Music USA program has long boasted the largest short-wave audience in all of Russia. I have never met any Russian under the age of twenty-five who has not heard it or is not familiar with it. Why?

Because day in and day out Music USA broadcasts the top of the U.S. hit parade, the big beat, the newest rock styles, the best of soul music. Whatever it is that young people are listening to anywhere in the world—Music USA is playing it. To paraphrase McLuhan—music is the message.

During the darkest years of Stalin when it literally meant risking exile to listen to "jazz," as Stalin called all Western music, Soviet youngsters managed to hear and play the latest Western hits, smuggled in from Berlin despite genuine peril of arrest and prison camp. The lure of Elvis Presley (in those days) was stronger than the fear of a term in the Kolyma gold fields.

Nothing spreads so rapidly as youth styles, youth mores, youth music, youth jargon, youth attitudes.

In recent years American visitors to Europe have been astounded to see tens of thousands of youngsters swarm in Piccadilly Circus and Hyde Park and equally large crowds clustering in the central parks and squares of Paris. Wherever you go you find throngs of youngsters, dressed alike in blue jeans, wearing their hair long, carrying woven Bulgarian shoulder bags or German knapsacks, sitting together, talking together, singing together, making love together. The American's initial impulse is that the young have all come from the East Village or the great campuses of the United States. But this is wrong. When you pass among the youngsters they are talking a dozen languages— English in the unmistakable accents of Yorkshire, American in the unmistakable accents of Texas, French, German, Polish, Dutch, Swedish, Italian, Greek—you name it. This is not an American invasion, it is a youth invasion, from every end of the world, and if you follow the trail around the globe the same thing can be seen in capital after capital, country after country—Istanbul, Beirut, Madras, Bangkok, Tokyo—wherever the planes, the trains, the buses, and the boats operate, the youth of the world is on the march, looking alike, talking alike, acting alike. At the time when Woodstock was happening in upper New York State there was a Dylan rally on the Isle of Wight. Clive Barnes attended Wight and he was struck by the fact that the people who came from all over Europe were not differentiated by nationality. "They dressed alike," he observed. "They even talked very similarly, almost with the same accent. The English kids and American kids have somehow developed a kind of mid-Atlantic Liverpudlian dialect of their own which is classless, Liverpudlian trans-Atlantic. . . ."

Hilton Kramer touched on a closely related phenomenon: "In the past three years I've been to São Paulo, Moscow, Leningrad, Prague, Berlin and other parts of western Europe, and wherever I go what people want to talk about is Mailer or Balanchine or Andy Warhol. It's not parochial to talk about these things. This is the world culture of advanced industrial nations. It's not the culture of African tribes or peasants on some plantation in Argentina. But it is the culture of advanced literate people the world over. . . ."

The world over. . . . Anyone who travels, anyone who observes the world, has seen this pervasiveness, this interrelationship of culture on all levels—the same films, possibly Polish, possibly French, possibly "blue" American; the same songs, almost invariably from the Liverpool crucible and its derivative centers in the United States; the same books, paperbacks from internationally based publishers, usually of American authorship (but sometimes of Russian, like Solzhenitsyn and Yevtushenko); the same styles of dress, the same dances, the same life-styles, the same emerging *Weltanschauung* (end-the-war, ban-the-bomb, freedom-for-all-peoples, end-discrimination, whether in Belfast, Glasgow, Harlem, or Kiev).

We have talked and talked and philosophized and philosophized about how modern communications have knit the world together. But we have been thinking in geopolitical terms, in communications terms, in economic terms. We have ignored the cultural unity of the world which is taking place under our own eyes. And nowhere more strikingly than in youth culture.

To be sure this is not new. A dozen years ago there were bopping gangs in Rotterdam; teenage gangs ranged the slums of Tokyo and assaulted each other with the same deadly violence as marked the battles of the Chaplains and the Bishops. England was the classic birthplace of almost all the life-styles of the youth. The zoot suit came out of the East End of London. The Teddy-boys gave the poor of Chicago's South Side a taste for velvet and purple and feathers. Edwardian chains and watch fobs originated in foggy London sidestreets. The granny dresses sprang from cockney origins to win a place all over the world as the badge of youth. French youngsters volunteered colored stockings and a taste for leather. Greenwich Village proposed mangy furs. Everywhere longer and longer hair became the mark of unity, the symbol of challenge to authority, and the cause for throwing young people into jail from the Navy brigs and Army stockades of the U.S.A. to the sweltering prison cages of Rawalpindi and Singapore.

Hair . . . this was the striking point, the trigger that set off explosion after explosion within families, within countries.

True, there were some citadels where signs of acculturation were minimal—the Soviet Union, the more remote parts of Eastern Europe (like Albania and Bulgaria but not Poland and Hungary), China, a continent unto itself, some of the high mountain tribes of central Asia, and the back jungles of Africa and Latin America.

All of this had been going on for years before America suddenly awakened to look about and ask the question of what was happening with American young people. The question was almost literally touched off by a single event (not that there had not been portentous shadows long before). It was touched off by Columbia, by the Columbia sit-in of the spring of 1968. The sit-in, the police bust, the first of innumerable instances of what came, in the words of the cliché, to be characterized as "police overreaction," happened then, and the American world awakened to what it thought it had never seen before—an aroused, politicized segment of its younger citizenry, strongly supported by other elements in the population, strongly and violently opposed by an equally formidable element of the populace.

What was it all about? Swiftly, almost simultaneously, there occurred the events of Paris, the flaring forth of student unrest and violent clashes with police and authority in widely separated parts of the world—in Berlin, in Rome, even in staid English institutions like the London School of Economics. The fever spread through the United States and rather belatedly we learned that armed clashes had been going on in Japan for several years between helmeted and caparisoned students and similarly armored Japanese security forces.

Immediately pundits and politicians undertook to generalize these phenomena—to erect a theory which would somehow embrace Red Rudi, Herbert Marcuse, Mark Rudd, and the Japanese Zengakuren. There *must* be, there *had* to be, some common line, some common cause-and-effect relationship. It was too coincidental that the outbreaks suddenly came at the same time. But the search for a common factor was tiresome and unproductive. Columbia had been touched off by a row over building a gym in a public park adjacent to the slums of Harlem. The French student difficulties had their origin in the hideous impersonality of Nanterre and spread to Paris by osmotic process. Marcuse, it turned out, was the hero of Red Rudi. But no one, or hardly anyone, among the students who made manifestations and manned barricades in his name had read his works—in fact, they had not even been translated into French at the time of the Paris troubles. As for the Japanese, we learned that the riots and armed manifestations between students and police had been under way for many years and involved wildly opposing groups (including at least four organizations, each of which professed to worship at the only *true* Communist shrine and which spent their time fighting one another when not fighting the police).

It was impossible to find common ground. All one could say was that, for uncertain reasons, young people in many parts of the world had grown violently restive. It was hardest to draw a parallel between the U.S. students and those of other lands, for basically only the Americans were affected by the Vietnam war, which was the underlying factor in their unrest, protest, and violent dissent. The war did not affect the French, the Germans, the English, or the Italians, or the Japanese. The puzzle became even more intractable if an effort was made to develop a hypothesis which would cover the student manifestations in China, the so-called Cultural Revolution and the Red Guard movement.

The distance between the Sorbonne student and Marcuse's thought was considerable, but the distance between the Columbia students and Mao's thought was unbridgeable. Nor was the problem made easier by the fad for Mao's little red book, the co-optation by many radical students of Mao as an icon, joining with those of Che Guevara, Fidel Castro, and Eldridge Cleaver. If no one had read Marcuse it was even more painfully evident that no one had read Mao. In fact the whole effort to string ideological lines between one student group and another, between one youth revolt and another, turned out to be bewilderingly futile. It was common to hear the expression "I'm an emotional Marxist" on the lips of a young man or young woman advocating the most extreme kinds of radical action or behavior. What this meant, of course, was that the young radical had never read a line of Marx. It was only after a year or two of blazing demonstrations, wild rhetoric, sit-ins, confrontations of every kind that some, probably a tiny handful, of young American rebels began gingerly to poke their noses into the works of their radical predecessors. But it could be demonstrated that few went very far in their study of Marx, Engels, Lenin, or Mao. Possibly Che Guevara was better read (he was more talked of), but almost none had ever heard of Georges Sorel, the philosophical ancestor of all anarchism, the philosopher whose theories so many were acting out.

What this means to me is that efforts to establish ideological connections between the various types and kinds of youth dissent are not only nonproductive but, in the favorite cliché of the generation, not relevant.

I do not mean that ideology and generalized principles have not begun to emerge out of the vast turmoil of the last three or four years. But I do not think it played much of a role in drawing young people into a common front against their elders.

The truth is that a full-scale revolt by the young was well under way before it began to spill over and out in manifestations like Columbia, like Nanterre, like the Zengakuren. It may be seen as a cyclical swing of a kind which is extremely common in human behavior. It first manifests itself in rebellion against old forms in areas extremely close to the young, extremely sensitive to change and style—music, dress, manners, mores, dancing, sex, eating, and recreation patterns.

A couple of years ago a little old lady, almost a classic example of the type, came up to me in Pittsburgh after I had given a talk about the international situation. "What you say is all very well," she said, "but I'll tell you who is really responsible for the state the world is in today—the Beatles." She meant it. She meant that the Beatles had stirred and stimulated a youth rebellion which had surged across cultural lines into social and political fields. I don't think that is the whole anwer but I think it comes a good deal closer than most answers.

Anyone looking back at his late teens knows how strong is the spirit of revolt, of experimentation, of upending the rules with which we are brought up (there are exceptions, in time and place, of course, as, for instance, in the U.S.A. during World War II). It is an atavistic thing. We all know, too, how strong at that age is the desire for togetherness, for camaraderie, to do, to act, to be the same as the rest of the crowd, particularly in any challenge of the rules.

It is not accidental, it seems to me, that the fiercest, most consistent, most persistent thrust of the young has been directed against that arm of social authority, that branch of the system which stands closest to them and which, in many instances, is a real parental surrogate—that is, the university authority. This has been almost universally true in Western countries. It is almost the only thread which ties the manifestations of Japanese students to those of Western countries. There is even a parallel to China, for there, too, in the earliest phase of the Red Guard movement, the targets were university and school authorities.

Thus, regardless of the different contents of the protest and dissent, the objective, at least, displayed similarity from country to country. And, just as young people struck first at what was nearest, closest, and (possibly) dearest to them, so as the battle became engaged it broadened to bring under fire a whole range of objects, institutions, and policies, for the most part objectives of a general nature and gradually assumed the form of a sharp challenge to basic and long-held concepts of the authority system, whether educational, familial, or governmental.

Thus, it is no accident that efforts to analyze these phenomena by classic Marxists led to disaster. Ask a good Russian Communist what he makes of the American "youth revolution." He responds, "What revolution?" If you persist (and I have), he may answer as did an old Moscow friend of mine:

"Really, we don't understand very well what your students are complaining about. They lead a very good life. They have better living conditions than young people anywhere in the world. We understand that most of these so-called revolutionaries are of bourgeois or upper-bourgeois origin. Frankly, this doesn't make any sense to us."

The same man was completely nonplussed by the confrontations between hard hats and young opponents of the war. "It's impossible," he said. "For proletarians to support the war and attack students and upper-class Wall Street brokers who oppose the war—how do you expect us to make head or tail of that?"

A serious Marxist, reviewing Jerry Rubin's *Do It!* and Abbie Hoffman's *Woodstock Nation*, helplessly exclaimed:

"When Abbie writes that he wants to go on trial 'not because I'm against corporate liberalism but because I think people should do whatever the fuck they want' he reveals the essential political paradox of all 'life style' revolution. That is: people have never been able to do 'whatever the fuck they want.'"

He concludes that "a crash course in Marxism would probably not have a significant effect on the nature of the radical movement in the U.S. today" and adds:

"The reason why 'life-style' revolution is non-Marxist, indeed, anti-Marxist is because Marxism is the scientific social philosophy of the revolutionary working class movement; and 'life-style' revolution, no matter what its rhetoric, attempts to define revolutionary change not by goals of the working class but by the values of the petty bourgeoisie."

Tom Hayden, perhaps the most philosophically inclined member of the Chicago Seven, incorporated an answer to such Marxist criticism in his book about the Chicago Conspiracy, called *The Trial.* Hayden wrote:

"Certainly, there is a gap between the children of affluence and the children of squalor. Our need for a new life style, for women's liberation, for the transformation of work, for a new environment and educational system, cannot be described in the rhetoric of the Third World revolution where poverty, exploitation and fascist violence are the immediate crisis. We cannot be black; nor can our needs be entrusted to a Third World vanguard of any kind.

"But our destiny and possible liberation cannot be separated from the Third World vanguards. The change toward which we are inevitably moving is one in which the white world yields

power and resources to an insistent mankind. There is no escape
—either into rural communes or existential mysticism—from this
dynamic of world confrontation."

There are many implications in Hayden's close-grained para-
graphs. But if I understand him correctly he is rejecting Marxism
in its narrow and principled definition; he is rejecting the dis-
ciplined Marxist parties of both the Communist world and the
so-called "Third World," and saying, in effect, that American
youth must create its own movement on as broad a front as
possible, doing its own thing in the closest collaboration with
other dissident movements, but conscious of its own identity
and its own birth in the particular circumstances of its age and
time and place.

Hayden accepts the "life-style" revolution, that is, the concept that what young people are about is a radical turnover not
only and even perhaps not principally in economic and political
relationships (although, of course, it quickly comes to that)
but basically in human relationships, the relationships of man
to man, of woman to woman, of men to women, of young to
old, of white to black to yellow to brown, of one ethnic group to
another. But not just in the U.S.A.—in the whole world. Thus,
Hayden, Hoffman, Rubin, and other articulate spokesmen of the
radical edge which was sharpened on the campus, in bloody confrontations, and in the Conspiracy trial accept the Liverpudlian
origin of youth mood and stance, synthesize it with antiwar, with
antistatism, antiracism, consumerism, environmentalism, and hope
that from this synthesis a new type of movement, differing from
any of the past or any now existing elsewhere in the world will
arise. Perhaps, indeed, they would insist that such a movement
has already been born. It is a messianic concept but its birthplace
is clearly located in what classic Marxists disparagingly call
"life-style" revolution.

Whether Hayden's thesis is valid, whether it may be possible that out of broad and originally generational dissent (a con-

cept Hayden strongly rejects) a radical leadership will emerge which possesses the unity, dynamism, direction, leadership, appeal, and strategy that will enable it to come to the top in this or any country, is an open question—one which only unfolding history can be expected to answer.

The fate of such a radical evolution probably will be determined within the United States. Nowhere else are the dialectics of power likely to favor its emergence. But its success in generalization, in effecting a change in the world environment of opinion so sweeping as to make a fundamental and transfiguring reconstitution of human society on a fully humane basis, will depend, it seems to me, on the validity of the idea that for the first time because of global intercultural penetration young people in every part of the world are moving in a recognizably similar pattern and quite possibly along a remarkably similar path.

CHAPTER 11

The
Credibility Gap

My reports from Hanoi in December, 1966, that American planes were hitting civilian targets, ordinary houses in Hanoi, peasant huts in the countryside, and even, occasionally, Catholic churches, causing heavy destruction and civilian deaths, created a worldwide sensation.

When I got back to America and discovered the extent of the uproar I was surprised. I am sure that it surprised the North Vietnamese and there is no doubt that it shocked many in the American military establishment.

The sensation has long since died away and there has been time enough for many, including some of the Pentagon spokesmen who were most vituperative, to reexamine the situation and draw a few conclusions. Not surprisingly they are almost identical with those which I drew at the time.

I said then and repeated the statement frequently that there was no logical reason for anyone to be shocked or surprised that American bombs were hitting nonmilitary targets and killing civilians in Vietnam. No reason, that is, for anyone who had the slightest familiarity with bombing either in World War II or subsequently. I myself had been through all the nonsense about "pinpoint" bombing with the RAF and the U.S. Eighth Air Force during World War II. The phrase used in those days to express the "accuracy" of strategic bombing was that it was "like shooting fish in a barrel." This was utter rot. Everyone knew that even with the Norden bombsight (an excellent sight but not nearly as accurate as the Air Force pretended) you could not count on many direct hits. Indeed, most of the time the bombers were not even attempting "pinpoint" attacks. They were doing area bombing, which is a euphemistic way of saying they were throwing the bombs down, say, on the northeast side of a town and hoping to get the power plant, the freight yards, and all the other stuff which were known to be located in that vicinity. But I never met a pilot (not even Curtis B. LeMay, who was only a colonel in those days and used to lead his own squadron into attack) who seriously thought that his bombs would not knock down non-military targets and kill civilians. No. No sophisticated person, no person who had been through World War II, no military man was ever in doubt that we were causing civilian casualties and nonmilitary destruction in North Vietnam. The only arguable point was whether we were killing civilians deliberately (as Hanoi rather naturally assumed) or only as a random side effect. A clear and straightforward military statement of the situation was made by Captain C. O. Holmquist in the *Naval Review* for 1969:

"Although many different types of unguided and guided air-to-ground weapons have been used by our attack aircraft in Vietnam, our principal weapon has been the same one used in World War II and Korea—the iron bomb. We have dropped more tonnage of ordnance in the Vietnamese conflict than in Europe during all World War II. Yet despite all this destruction, our efforts to date to deter the enemy with bombs appear less than successful.

"Much of the iron bomb tonnage we have dropped has use-lessly cratered rice paddies or exploded harmlessly in the jungle foliage. The repeated sorties required to hit pinpoint targets with bombs have given the Communist gunners a field day. Our high combat losses have been caused mostly by small arms fire and anti-aircraft guns.

"One naturally wonders why so many bombing sorties are re-quired in order to destroy a bridge or other pin-point target. . . .

"With even the most sophisticated computer system, bomb-ing by any mode remains an inherently inaccurate process, as is evident from our results to date in Vietnam. Aiming errors, bore-sight errors, system computational errors and bomb dispersion errors all act to degrade the accuracy of the system. Unknown winds at altitudes below the release point and the 'combat de-gradation' factor add more errors to the process. In short, *it is impossible to hit a small target with bombs except by sheer luck. Bombing has proved most efficient for area targets such as supply dumps, built-up areas, and cities*" (my italics).

I think anyone familiar with the actuality of bombing would agree that this is an objective statement of the problem. If you add the fact that on many missions into North Vietnam the bombs were actually released (as has since become known) not by the pilots at all but by computers activated by intricate and complex mechanisms sited in north Laos or Thailand, you can see why, as Holmquist laconically notes, "bombing by any mode re-mains an inherently inaccurate process."

Moreover, there were other factors, more cynical, less hap-hazard, at work—the competition between Air Force and Navy for primacy in air missions and "delivered" bomb tonnage, the com-petition between commanders and carriers for volume of missions and between squads and individual units for successful comple-tion of assignments. It was this, no doubt, that gave rise to the monstrous random bombing incidents—the casual release of bombs over the countryside rather than bringing them back to base or carrier when primary targets proved unhittable because of fog or other cause, the jettisoning of bombs on secondary or alternative targets, often of the most marginal definition even by intelligence calculation, the wholesale use of so-called "suppressive" bombing and gunfire, the vagabond concept of "free fire zones" in which the pilots literally could do anything they wished —any moving or stationary object being considered a "fair" target.

So . . . all this being so, why the static, why the hullabaloo, why the national outrage, the international excitement when I reported the plain, the obvious, the inevitable?

Simple. The Pentagon and President Johnson, unquestionably wishing to soft-pedal the bombing act, had again and again issued statements and spoken publicly to give the impression that the only targets of American bombs were "steel and concrete," that by some miracle of science we were now actually able to direct our explosives onto the antiaircraft gun platforms, blow them up, kill the gunners, and never hurt the children playing in the grass hut 100 yards away.

It was, of course, in the clear but crude words of the Army, nothing but a crock. But because people are trained and conditioned to believe the President, to believe the Government (and perhaps because we have a childlike faith in technology and really don't *want* to believe that we are waging a war in which innocent men, women, and children are falling victim to our bombs, bullets, and fire chemicals), it certainly *was* believed. So when my reports and photos showing, beyond question, that the cheery, rosy, hazy picture of the white-jacket war, the gently surgical war in which only "steel and concrete" and an occasional Bad Guy was being killed, had no more basis in fact than an opium fiend's nightmare, there was hell to pay. At long last someone had noticed that the Emperor was not wearing clothes and had pointed out this curious fact to the mulitude. Not all the indignation felt by the government publicity men was directed against myself (although this was carefully concealed at the time). As one of the Pentagon propagandists, Phil Goulding, has since made plain in his book *Confirm or Deny,* a considerable portion was directed toward their chiefs and to some extent against themselves. For there were those who had anticipated a day of reckoning but not necessarily precisely the one which arrived.

As Goulding says:

"There occurred another series of events with which I was involved intimately and which constituted, in my view, the biggest public affairs mistake of the McNamara-Clifford regimes. . . .

"It is my belief that our failure in this instance contributed markedly to the public distrust of the government which welled up in the mid- and late 1960s, particularly but not exclusively in regard to government statements on Vietnam.

"The subject was the bombing of North Vietnam; the mistake was the failure of President Johnson's administration to explain to the citizens of the United States that our bombing inevitably was destroying homes and killing civilians. We permitted the impression to spread that the bombing operations of U.S. aircraft were executed with such surgical precision that we had dropped bombs only on military targets. And when the nation suddenly discovered, largely through the writing of Harrison E. Salisbury of the *New York Times,* that homes were being destroyed in the North and that civilians were being killed, the nation's reaction was a traumatic one.

"While additional loss of faith in the word of the government was the dominant part of that reaction, another part was deeper disenchantment with the war itself."

If this had been the only gaff, the only observed, documented, publicly authenticated discordance between what the government said and what the government did, if this was the only certified occasion in which Public Policy differed from Public Statement by the President, the Secretary of State, the Secretary of Defense, the Joint Chiefs, I do not think the consequences would have been so traumatic.

But it was not. It came after the public had observed time after time after time enormous divergences between the reality they perceived and the reality described by their Leaders. And it was this circumstance which made the exposure of the lie about steel-and-concrete so devastating.

Again and again Westmoreland had reported to President Johnson, who gladly shared this confidence with the public, that "there is light at the end of the tunnel" or that the "war has turned the corner." Again and again McNamara made the ritual 72-hour trip to Saigon, the Big Trip in the great computerized Air Force Special, leaving Washington in early morning, pausing at Honolulu for the ceremonial meeting with the man who really runs the war—CINCPAC, the Pacific Commander in Chief—flying on for the 8 A.M. arrival in Saigon, the day-long briefing in the video-colored auditorium, the sacramental Trip-to-the-Field, the return to Washington to issue the Optimistic Communiqué, the contents of which had been generally agreed upon before the plane ever took off on its 8,000-mile flight across the Pacific and back.

Time and again Mr. Johnson shared with the American public his optimism, his certainty, his sunny vision of the future.

But never did any of this come true. And while, as P. T. Barnum discovered, you can fool some of the people all of the time and all of the people some of the time, you can never fool all of the people all of the time. Month by month and year by year the number who could be fooled on Vietnam (and God knows the people *wanted* to believe in LBJ and the nearing end of the war) grew smaller and smaller.

What I am saying is simply this: By the time I reported the simple, obvious, inevitable, predictable, conventional, expectable, routine news that American bombs were killing civilians and knocking down nonmilitary targets in Hanoi, the critical point had been reached at which the public was prepared to turn against the sludge of optimistic lies which it had been fed. After several years it no longer believed that Mr. Johnson was a latter-day Dr. Coué, although, perhaps, until my reports from Hanoi came in it had continued to repeat ritually that every day in every way the war was going better and better.

Unfortunately, or fortunately, depending on your viewpoint, this transformation of the public attitude toward Washington's credibility (for the transformation affected not just LBJ; we can readily see that the public skepticism embraced all of Washington) came after previous events had badly shaken its confidence.

The assassination of President Kennedy shocked the popular psyche so savagely that it has by no means recovered to this day, and the trauma has been heightened by the subsequent assassinations of Bobby and Dr. King. The public, Warren Commission or no, has never really accepted the official account of John F. Kennedy's death. It probably never will. The tragedy was so great; the cause, seemingly so trivial. When Kings, Great Men, and Presidents die our minds and hearts cry out for Great Reasons. Oswald and Jack Ruby were figures so banal, so trite, so petty that we compulsively seek (in the multitude of conspiratorial theories) explanations more grand or at least more grandiose.

Thus, our confidence in Washington was already badly undermined. The steady escalation of the gap between word and reality on Vietnam stretched confidence to the breaking point. Once it broke it would not easily be restored. Indeed, the restoration has not occurred under Nixon.

This is not a new phenomenon, although it seems to most of us to be new. The last time it happened on a national scale was during the Great Depression. It was Mr. Hoover's fate to be saddled with the same withdrawal of public confidence and it stemmed from an identical cause—his repeated statements that prosperity was just around the corner, that the country was fundamentally sound, that economic conditions were improving. When these statements were received by the ordinary citizen who had been six months out of a job, who was losing his house because

he could not make the mortgage payments, who saw the bread-
lines outside the Salvation Army each time he made the hopeless
rounds looking for work, who knew that more and more factories
in his hometown not only were laying off men but were actually
closing down—Mr. Hoover began to lose credibility. Once this
corrosive process set in there was nothing the President could
do—except what he was unwilling to do. If Mr. Hoover had
abandoned his Pollyanna pose (or had Mr. Johnson done the
same), he could have taken the first steps back to credence and
acceptability. But this, of course, would have been to admit the
worst—and few presidents are willing to do this, lacking the kind
of courage which John Kennedy demonstrated in publicly taking
full responsibility for the Bay of Pigs fiasco on his own shoulders.

Once credibility is lost it sometimes cannot be regained.
Governments and presidents never seem to learn this lesson. How
many times have I heard a Russian say, "I read it in *Pravda*—
so of course it isn't true." The oldest joke in Moscow is the hoary
one about *Pravda* and *Izvestiya,* the two big newspapers. *Izvestiya* means News and *Pravda* means Truth. The Moscow joke is,
There is no Truth in *Pravda* and there is no News in *Izvestiya.*
Like all good jokes this one is founded on grim reality. After
being conditioned to *Pravda* and *Izvestiya* for many years, I now
read the Soviet newspapers as my Russian friends do—not for
what the papers say but for what they don't say. The omissions
are what count. Or I observe what they say about a situation and
deduce, with my Russian friends, that the reality is precisely
the reverse. This, of course, occasionally leads Russians to completely wrong conclusions. Occasionally, an article in *Pravda*
happens to be true. But this is an inescapable hazard. If you
follow the rule of thumb that the world picture is just about the
opposite of *Pravda's* report you will be much closer to being
right than if you accept *Pravda* as word-for-word accurate.

Here, of course, we have the key to the counterproductivity
of propaganda and the reason why, contrary to all dismal pre-

dictions by the social scientists, the Communist agitprops have
not succeeded in turning the Russians into a nation of robots
who react precisely the way the Kremlin computers predict and
anticipate. The heart of the matter is the gap between perceived
reality and *Pravda*'s version of reality. George Creel, the first
American propaganda director (during World War I), formulated
a basic concept which might well be called Creel's Rule. It is
simply this: No propaganda can be effective unless it is consistent with reality and the truth. In other words, you cannot turn
a bad situation into a good one by calling it good. It may work
once but the next time you try it a certain number of people will
not buy your version. Once bitten twice shy.

We know this instinctively in our personal life; why contemporary governments, whether in Washington or Moscow, don't
recognize this fact I don't know. Nowhere to my knowledge has
the long corrosion of credibility been more deeply felt than in
the Soviet Union. Especially does the Soviet government find it
impossible to muster strong support when it comes to the American
question—the counterconditioning has gone too far. The Russians
are like Pavlov's dogs. At first the dogs salivated at the sound of
a bell when they were fed. Feeding was then withdrawn and
they continued to salivate at the sound of the bell. But eventu-
ally, food not being forthcoming, they stopped salivating at the
bell and it was not possible to reactivate the reaction.

So it is with the Russian public. A Soviet correspondent in
the United States had great difficulty in 1970 reporting on the
economic downturn. His editors felt he was exaggerating. They
refused to let him call it a "recession" and were adamant against
comparisons with a "depression." A Soviet friend of mine laughed
at this and said, "You must understand. For fifty years our papers
have been predicting every day that the American economy was
about to collapse. But it never has. So even if we were to report
it this time—and even if it was true—nobody in Russia would believe it."

The U.S.A. has not reached the position of Russian as regards credibility. But in our own way we have entered a period of intense skepticism toward information from ordinarily recognized authorities. The credibility gap affects not only Washington, the presidency, important government spokesmen, and the military. It affects the great information media—the newspapers, the news magazines, the television networks. There is a spreading to the media of the distrust which the public feels for all sources of information. But there is another element, as well. Much of the news reported these days is unpleasant, disturbing, depressing. It reports events which many people do not wish to hear about or even to admit are happening—the horror of American atrocities in Vietnam, the savagery of police officers, the riots of the blacks, the students, the dissidents. This is a difficult diet for anyone. It is too much for some and the "shoot the messenger" syndrome sets in—the classic Roman pattern of slaying the herald who arrives with bad news—blaming the media rather than society.

We cannot agree on what the truth is and we establish separate and contradictory truths. A typical and endlessly repeated example is the tug of war which breaks out whenever a great demonstration occurs in Washington. Supporters wish to magnify the event, opponents to minimize it. The symbol of the struggle usually is the size of the crowd. Supporters believe it to number 500,000. Detractors put the figure at 100,000. A newspaper carefully calculates the total as 300,000. Everyone's anger flares at the paper. Demonstrators contend it is biased against their cause; opponents contend it is playing into the hands of the demonstration. The net result is a loss of credibility.

In fact, partisans reject the whole notion of "objectivity" and factualness. President Nixon's supporters insist that television and the press have no right to report a presidential error or misstatement, such as the President's declaration that Charles Manson was guilty of seven or eight murders. In their view the remark should have been suppressed or corrected. During the Barry

Goldwater campaign of 1964 his advocates again and again attacked the press and TV—not for misreporting Goldwater's statements or for failure to report them but for another crime—for reporting *exactly* what Goldwater said. The press, in their view, should either have suppressed Goldwater's misstatements or corrected them.

Many college graduates, particularly editors of college publications and journalism majors, instead of seeking positions on the great American newspapers or with the television networks have turned their backs on commercial journalism. What they want is advocacy, not impartiality—a concept which they reject on its premise. They do not believe that news can be reported without bias and they have no interest in such an aseptic occupation. They are partisans, through and through, and they propose to devote their energies to campaigning for causes in which they believe.

The credibility gap may be analyzed from many vantage points. But it is plain from this cursory summary that it is deep and pervasive in the United States. It continues to deepen and spread. It exists not in isolation. It is not simply a problem of disbelief in what Mr. Nixon says or what *The New York Times* or Walter Cronkite reports. It is a symptom of disbelief in and skepticism toward the whole environment of America. Institutions like the presidency, the government in Washington, the great information media, the universities, the Church are keystones of the American system. The erosion of public confidence in them means not only that whatever the President says or the newspaper reports is not believed by large segments of the public. It means that to large segments of the public—and the cross-section runs from the wildest fringes of the Weathermen through the solid small-town middle class to the wildest fringes of those who regard the Birchites as overly liberal—basic elements in the American system are suspect. What has really happened it this: In losing confidence in the integrity of the pillars of the American system we have, in essence, lost confidence not only in the system but in ourselves. Thus, when we talk of a credibility gap, what we really mean is not only that we do doubt Mr. Nixon, Mr. Johnson, General Westmoreland, *Time* magazine, Huntley-Brinkley. We do not believe, despite our passionate protestations to the contrary, in our country and its traditional system. We do not believe in ourselves.

CHAPTER 12

The Military-Industrial Complex

A decade has passed since President Eisenhower's warning against the influence of what he called the military-industrial complex. It was a warning so prescient, so apt, so far-seeing that hardly a day has passed without someone on a high public platform invoking the President's words. But, alas, each day has witnessed the growth more intense and extensive in the influence of those forces against which General Eisenhower's words were directed.

Indeed, it is almost certainly the growth in weight and prestige of the military-industrial complex—and this almost alone—which has so crushingly distorted the normal functioning of government in the United States.

We have become accustomed to the enormous figures of the military budget—the 70-odd billions for the "defense establishment," roughly half the national budget, and the 25 to 30 billions for the Vietnam war. We, perhaps, do not realize that the "defense" total has almost *doubled* since President Eisenhower's declaration of January 17, 1961, or that of the 44.6 billion we

spent on the military in the last Eisenhower 1960–61 budget of
100 billion, the amount for Vietnam was so tiny that the figure
wasn't even reported. We may not fully realize how the remorse-
less growth of the military cancer has twisted our country and
government into a painful grotesque enormously devoted to feeding the military-industrial oligarchs.

Money is power—particularly in Washington—as every effort
to reduce the extraordinary weight of the military budget has
demonstrated. Money is power because the military spends hundreds of millions in almost every state and in some states they
spend billions. Money is jobs—thousands, tens of thousands, hundreds of thousands, millions. Military jobs mean the difference between prosperity and depression in cities like San Diego, Seattle,
Wichita, East Hartford, and many many more. In President
Eisenhower's last year the Defense Establishment numbered
about 3,500,000, of whom 2,467,000 were in the Armed Forces.
As of July 1, 1970, the Establishment numbered 4,643,000, of whom
3,440,000 were in the Armed Forces. The number of men and
women employed in private industry who are engaged in defense
projects is so vast that not even the Defense Department is prepared to estimate the total. All it can say is that in the two years
between June, 1969, and June, 1971, it hopes to cut 1,641,000 persons from the payroll, including 682,000 in the Armed Forces
and about 900,000 in private industry.

President Nixon has sliced off only the thinnest salami from
the tremendous military porkus—possibly 5 billion dollars, perhaps
7 percent of the total. He hopes to achieve that in fiscal 1970–
1971 by cutting spending from 80 billion (8 or 9 percent of Gross
National Product or 37.79 percent of the total budget) to 76.6
billion dollars (about 7 percent of GNP or 34.6 percent of the
national budget). Even with cuts of so small a percentile the
effect across the economy has been a minor earthquake. For all
the bright talk of the economists, genuine cutbacks, real reduc-
tions in the arms budget, obviously would produce a temporary

depression or worse.

We are all vaguely aware of these figures but they are too big to mean much. What we also don't understand is the kind of philosophy, the kind of establishment, which has grown up behind that single word: Pentagon.

Take one area. We suppose that our foreign policy is conducted by the State Department as conceived and defined by the White House in collaboration with the Secretary of State. When something goes wrong in Pakistan or Venezuela we blame the diplomats.

The reality is far different. The strongest influence in U.S. foreign policy is the military establishment, not State, not the CIA, not even the White House. Nor is this new or recent. If you look at George Kennan's study of U.S. policy at the end of World War II, at the low-profile, ineffective role played by State during World War II and the intractability of the military when State tried gingerly and futilely to reassert its constitutional prerogatives, you begin to get a glimmer of the overpowering influence which the Pentagon now has.

The dominance of the military in policy-making is not conducted on an ad hoc basis. There has grown up in the Pentagon what amounts to a complete "state department" which maintains its own foreign relations, its own policy studies, its own intelligence, its own extremely effective liaison with the White House and those key individuals in Congress necessary for its operations. It has an enormous publicity and propaganda apparatus reaching down to the tiniest radio stations and weekly newspapers, an enormous lobbying apparatus, thrown into action on something like SST or ABM. It can orchestrate a national pressure drive with a sophistication such as no other organization can match (utilizing the resources of its thousands of contractors, subcontractors, suppliers, provisioners, raw-materials producers in every state with their web of local, state, and national economic and political connections); it can blackmail or reward to the tune of billions of

dollars; its favor can elect, though not always defeat, a Senator
and ruin a great bank; it can assure a corporation executive his
six-figure stock bonus; it can send a billion-dollar manufacturer
to the wall; it looks after its own, retiring an endless procession
of money-hungry generals and colonels into military-supply corporations where they quickly enrich themselves.

In the foreign field the military have—or seem to have—every
possible advantage. They pick, train, and cozen promising military of other countries (thus, hopefully ensuring endlessly symbiotic relationships and a mutuality not only of interest but of
viewpoint); they have boundless quantities of military (and nonmilitary) goods to shower down on their favorites, either at no
cost or at bargain rates (and no questions asked, or almost none,
if the recipient turns a handsome resale profit). Art Buchwald's
caricature in *Sheep on the Runway* of the Pentagon arms dis-
penser with his catalogue of give-away goodies ranging from
supersonic fighter-bombers to walk-in PX's is only slightly exag-
gerated. They train foreign armies and nourish the rise of
military dictatorships (it is the despair of the military and their
companions in the intelligence establishment that so many promising, well-rewarded, well-trained colonels, in the end, wind up
pursuing nationalistic anti-American policies like the late Colonel
Nasser. But, of course, there can always be another coup d'état).

Thus, State may *say* or may even *think* that it makes U.S.
policy vis-à-vis Country A in Latin America or Country Y in Asia.
The military don't mind—so long as the reality is theirs. It is the
reality that counts—the reality of endless contracts, profits, and
jobs. And these contracts are usually the best kind of contracts—
the lovely cost-plus variety so that there is never any loss—just a
question of how much profit can be extracted. If there is a mis-
calculation on costs there can always be a nice "overrun" and a
new supplemental appropriation. Or if Congress wants to show
off and pretend for the benefit of the taxpayer that it is watching
the dollars—well, then there can be penalties. But on the next

deal (and there is always a next deal) the contract can be carefully sweetened so that no one loses or is out of pocket except you
and me, the great American suckers, the taxpayers who support
this hideous, ridiculous, bloated, self-perpetuating, self-rewarding
monstrosity.

In former days there have been great military establishments,
although not in the U.S.A., and they have always, invariably, and
without exception led to the downfall of the country in which
they rose. (Caesar's, Alexander's, Genghis Khan's, Napoleon's, the
Kaiser's, and Hitler's, to cite a few classic cases. Spengler believed
that "Caesarism" was civilization's fatal lust orgy before the
Gotterdammerung.) We never had a big, permanent, continuing
military establishment until after World War II. Before that we
had our arms lobbies and our military industries, but they were
small, and recurrent scandals kept them in line, like the juicy
Zakharoff exposés of the late 1920s and the "merchants of death"
inquiry.

Moreover, the government in order to prevent profit-making
and self-serving links between military and industry ran its own
big ordinance works—the huge naval shipyards and all the rest.
We had a tradition, however ill-kept, of a citizen soldiery, of a
militia which would spring into being at a moment's notice.
Military service was glorified in wartime, despised in peacetime.
The clutter of forts and old Indian-fighting bases scattered over
the country, largely in the West, was regarded, quite rightly, by
the local citizenry as harmless boondogglery, although a Congressman could always win merit by demanding that some fort (other
than one in his district) be abandoned as a waste to the taxpayers.

Fort Snelling, Minnesota, during my childhood in Minneapolis was a classic example of such an institution—a western fort
established to hold pioneer territory against the Sioux but preserved for the benefit of a small group of indolent officers and their
"troops." It was, of course, vastly expanded to train troops in

World War I but quickly shrank back after the war and, so far as I know, did little beyond maintaining a third-class polo team during the interwar period. It was the subject of repeated and very sensible agitation to close down but, of course, it never did. It survived into World War II, again to be expanded as a training base, and even persisted into the 1970s for God knows what reason, although the bulk of its facilities long since have been taken over by the Veterans Administration.

But if Fort Snelling prior to World War II was a good example of the useless expenditure persisted in by the military establishment, it is not even a symbolic representation of the problem which has grown up in the postwar years. The installations, the expenditures, the waste have escalated until the imaginations of ordinary persons can no longer comprehend their magnitude. Today it isn't a question of old Indian forts in the U.S.A. It is a question of billion-dollar establishments in countries whose location most of us could not even find on the globe and for purposes which, in all probability, not many of us would understand, even if the military bothered to explain them.

But the rule of the military remains the same: never give up a post; never give up a function because the larger the permanent establishment the more generals there can be, the more colonels, the more captains, and the higher the brilliant commander as well as the stupidest timeserver can rise in the ranks to early well-paid retirement.

This has a grievous bearing on the Vietnam war. It is too early yet to analyze with exactitude the influence at each critical phase which selfish military interests have played (I mean the interests of an establishment-in-being, not genuine national defense, strategic or tactical interest; interests connected with interservice rivalry, aggrandizement of individual organizations, career considerations, defense-contractor relationships). But a few have floated to the surface. There is no doubt, for example, that the Marine Corps has had no business whatever operating in Vietnam on a permanent basis. It is an elite corps, specially designed to carry out firefighting duties, to dash ashore, seize a beachead, and hold it for the follow-up detachments. It has no other purpose. It is not trained or equipped to fight long and large-scale engagements deep in the interior of a tropical country. This it has done in Vietnam, occasionally with brilliant success and occasionally with enormous and probably avoidable losses and great cost. The reason, I strongly suspect, has been to give the Marines a part of the action, to enable the corps to score at the expense of other branches of the military. And what do you suppose the Naval Air Force is doing fighting a land war in Vietnam? Well, if the Naval Air Force was not there, if the carrier-based aviation had not been flung into the battle, what role would there have been for the Navy? Some peanut PT patrols in the Mekong or off the coast? Right. The Navy wasn't going to get squeezed out. It is a bright, tough, energetic, highly competitive outfit. It commands the Pacific from Honolulu and to the Navy that practically means the world.

The truth is that technology has virtually made the whole concept of the Navy and Mahan's great doctrine of naval power obsolete. The battleship has followed the dinosaur into desuetude; the attack carrier is as obsolete as the dodo, except for use against primitive native or guerrilla enemies who can't use air power to hit back at vulnerable floating parking lots; naval troop transport (except in limited cases) long since has been outmoded by huge troop planes; only the nuclear submarines retain, for a time, their validity as a military force. One of the most pathetic of naval maneuvers in Vietnam was the hideously costly refitting of the old dreadnaught *New Jersey* as a gun platform to be used, it was claimed, to rocket-bombard North Vietnam from the sea. The old hulk, as crowded with long-range launchers as a chicken coop with hens, was trundled out to the Pacific and then hauled back to the U.S. without firing a shot. After spending a hundred million on the project, even the Navy couldn't believe in the *New Jersey's* credibility. No one quite understood what motivated the operation besides profitable refitting deals and sentiment for the good old days of the unsinkables. Some suspected the *Jersey* actually was destined to become a modern *Maine*—certainly had she been sunk by land-based ground-to-ground Soviet missiles, as not a few observers predicted, the national outcry would have made the Hearst-Pulitzer to-do over the sinking of the *Maine* seem like small-time vaudeville.

The plain truth is that in the Vietnam war the Army's own aviation is the one integral air ingredient which is effective in jungle guerrilla operations. What is needed is close support bombing and strafing, swift strikes on enemy rockets, enemy artillery, enemy attacking units, swift and enormously effective helicopter gun platforms and helicopter services, bringing in reserves, taking out wounded, all done in the quickest, closest collaboration with the field commanders.

Had the war in Vietnam been fought with strict military logic, there would have been no Marines (except, possibly, for an initial phase), no carrier aircraft, and no B-52's. Before President Johnson gave the order to bomb North Vietnam, the strategic Air Force had no role in the war at all. No Guam-based B-52's, for God's sake, and none in Thailand. Did the fact that the strategic Air Force had been frozen out of the action have anything to do with inside lobbying for the big strikes in the North? You write your guess on a piece of paper and put it in a sealed envelope. I'll do the same. And I'll venture that the guesses turn out identical— no matter what the official record shows.

Over this incredibly unpopular war in Asia there has always loomed an enormous albatross—the albatross of declarations by one American general after another—Eisenhower, MacArthur, Ridgeway, Clark, Wedemeyer (you name him and he belongs on the list)—counseling that whatever happens America must never get involved in a protracted, extended land war in Asia. They all excepted Korea as the one which could not be avoided (but which was halted as soon as a military man got into the White House). But they have been adamant on the general principle.

This classic American doctrine overhangs the U.S. military establishment. It overhangs Vietnam. It cannot be explained away or rationalized. Perhaps, this is what has given rise to a new, not completely articulated but nonetheless emerging doctrine—the doctrine of the "capital-intensive," personnel-limited war. It is fought with ingenious (and costly) machines and equipment rather than large numbers of Americans. It is this theoretical concept which lay behind McNamara's thinking; his investment of billions in the so-called electronic trip-line which was to seal off North Vietnam and even the Ho Chi Minh trail; the use of incredibly expensive and delicate electronic and infra-red (and other security-restricted means) to sense, to smell, to spot enemy activity of every kind; the employment of computerized techniques for selecting bombing targets and for actual bombing; of unmanned drone planes for reconnaissance; of electronic reconnaissance; of every kind of machine and engine which the extraordinary American technological establishment can devise in order to replace U.S. men; the use of technology to fight a war, minimizing U.S. casualties, maximizing enemy casualties.

That, indeed, is the kind of war, more or less, that we have increasingly developed in Vietnam. True, we have had to employ 500,000 U.S. men to make it go. True, 40,000 Americans have lost their lives. But now the casualty rate is coming down radically.

The use of capital-intensive tactics implies other techniques, too. For example, rendering the countryside noninhabitable (napalm, defoliants, desiccants, soil-poisoners) so that the "sea" in which the guerrillas "swim" becomes a vacant desert. This means, of course, that civilian populations (in the South, in Laos, possibly in Cambodia) must be herded into "Resettlement," "Pacification," "Rehabilitation" centers. For those euphemisms read, Concentration camps. In other words, if we round up the surviving people and put them behind barbed wire and use our technology to destroy the countryside, the enemy cannot operate in those areas. (Sorry, chums. To save the country we have had to destroy it.)

I suspect it is the calculated shift to what I call capital-intensive war (machines not men) which has given the Vietnam war such a depersonalized aura. This is not a war of men. How seldom do we read of individuals, either on our side or the other? What name on the Hanoi side is known besides Ho Chi Minh? Possibly, General Giap, but I should think his recognition factor is very, very low. And what of "our own" Vietnamese? They, too, are faceless men, invisible men, with the exception of Generals Thieu and Ky (of course, some of us still remember the ill-fated Diem and Madame Nhu). It is not like other wars, even the Korean, in which we saw our allies as real people. We sorrowed for the poor Korean orphans, we wept over pictures of the Korean women refugees in long white gowns and the men with quaint hats and beards. But who has seen a South Vietnamese refugee? Who has befriended a South Vietnamese child? Who has heard a Vietnamese poet speak or a Vietnamese singer chant the lays of his ancient land? Who knows the art of these suffering people who we have spent hundreds of billions of our treasure and thousands of our lives to "aid"? Who knows their history? Who tells their story? Who prints their pictures except for that image repeated again and again of the GI carrying a wounded child or helping a hobbling woman to escape the flame and bomb?

It is as though we were waging war in a dream, in a country which does not exist, helping people whose presence is only recorded on film or paper. The flesh and blood is not there. Since the war started hardly one live Vietnamese, outside of military and diplomats, has visited the country. To those who remember the suffering Belgians of World War I, the gallant British of World War II, the refugees from Hungary, from Cuba, and long ago from Armenia and Russia it seems unimaginable that we have fought for ten years without even learning how to pronounce the name of the land we are "rescuing."

The capital-intensive war is just one of the self-serving rationales which have been born in the great hippodrome of the American "defense establishment." (To me it seems much more honest to call it, as we did before the ill-fated amalgamation, the "War Department"; after all that's what it was, is, and always will be. To call it "defense" has an Orwellian ring; so does the pseudomotto of the Air Force: "Peace is our Profession." Some profession! Some peace!)

If half the money the government spends is being spent by the military, if the military is the largest employer in government, if the military has at its disposal the largest number of jobs in the civilian economy, if the military is (often) the largest single contributor to the budget of a foreign state or foreign dictator, is it any wonder that its influence pervades not only the government but the whole American ethos? Of course it does. We resent (and I personally resent) the assertion which so many foreigners make that the United States has become the military dictator of the world. It has not. But it could be. And it would not have to change much. The military could accomplish this from the sanctuary of the Pentagon which it now occupies.

Pause and look back to the words of our greatest military commander of modern times, Dwight David Eisenhower. Listen to him again, speaking in that bumbling, halting, un-oratorical Kansas voice, in his Farewell Address of January 17, 1961, three days before he was to hand over the office to John Fitzgerald Kennedy:

"Crises there will continue to be. In meeting them, whether foreign or domestic, great or small, there is a recurring temptation to feel that some spectacular and costly action could become the miraculous solution to all current difficulties. A huge increase in newer elements of our defense; development of unrealistic programs to cure every ill in agriculture; a dramatic expansion in basic and applied research. . . .

"But each proposal must be weighed in the light of broader consideration; the need to maintain balance in and among national programs. . . .

"The record of many decades stands as proof that our people and their government have, in the main, understood these truths and have responded to them well, in the face of stress and threat. But threats, new in kind or degree, constantly arise. I mention two only.

"A vital element in keeping the peace is our military establishment. Our arms must be mighty, ready for instant action, so that no potential aggressor may be tempted to risk his own destruction.

"Our military organization today bears little relation to that known by any of my predecessors in peacetime or indeed by the fighting men of World War II or Korea.

"Until the latest of our world conflicts, the United States had no armaments industry. American makers of plowshares could, with time and as required, make swords as well. But now we can no longer risk emergency improvisation of national defense; we have been compelled to create a permanent armaments industry of vast proportions. Added to this three and a half million men and women are directly engaged in the defense establishment. We annually spend on military security more than the net income of all United States corporations.

"This conjugation of an immense military establishment and a large arms industry is new in the American experience. The total influence—economic, political, even spiritual—is felt in every city, every State House, every office of the Federal government. We recognize the imperative need for this development. Yet we must not fail to comprehend its grave implications. Our toil, resources, and livelihood are all involved; so is the very structure of our society.

"In the councils of government, we must guard against the acquisition of unwarranted influence whether sought or unsought by the military-industrial complex. The potential for the disastrous rise of misplaced power exists and will persist.

"We must never let the weight of this combination endanger our liberties or democratic process. We should take nothing for granted. Only an alert and knowledgeable citizenry can compel the proper meshing of the huge industrial and military machinery of defense with our peaceful methods and goals so that security and liberty may prosper together."

So ten years ago Dwight Eisenhower stated the question, the threat, the need. No one could say it better. The whole problem is there. Ten years have passed. The words are more poignant, more pressing. Ten years later the military-industrial complex has grown so huge that many Americans (and many more of our friends and enemies abroad) gravely fear that the "disastrous rise of misplaced Power" has already occurred, and among those who do not share this belief the fear is growing that unless the Vietnam catastrophe can be speedily ended the disaster of which Mr. Eisenhower warned will become inevitable and there will, indeed, arise in the world an American military empire, triumphant at home and unassailable (except by mutual nuclear catastrophe) abroad.

It is this rampant, gangrenous, virtually unchecked military development which underlies the national crisis. So long as it is not perceived, so long as the headlong rush toward military autarchy is not halted, the national crisis will persist.

CHAPTER 13

On Revolutionary Morals

When I was an undergraduate at the University of Minnesota I took a course one semester from a Russian emigré professor whose name meant nothing to me and whose English was so primitive that it was often quite impossible to understand what subject he had selected for the day's lecture, let alone what he was saying. Actually, so far as I could make out, this was not important because what he was talking about, most of the time, were his narrow escapes from death in the course of fleeing Bolshevik Russia. The professor's name was Pitirim A. Sorokin, and he was very well known, I later discovered, in Russia, having been the youngest member of the Kerensky cabinet. Soon thereafter he went on to Harvard and a distinguished career in the field of philosophy and social thought.

The title of Sorokin's course at Minnesota was, I believe, "The Theory of Revolution," and while, in reality, it was mostly the history of his own revolution, he did introduce one concept which I remember very well. This was a distinction between a revolution and a mere revolt or coup d'état. In the category of revolutions Sorokin placed the French and the Russian. The American revolution he classified as falling somewhat short of classic although he was willing to concede that it was more than a mere "revolt."

What characterized a true revolution, to Sorokin's way of thinking, was the profundity of the overturn—a revolution meant not just a change in rulers, a change, say, in governmental forms, but also a change in philosophy, a change in the names of institutions and in the character of the institutions, a change in the way men regarded themselves and the world, a change of philosophy as well as of organization.

I think that by Sorokin's definition there has been since that time one more genuine revolution, the Chinese Revolution. I rather think that he would exclude all the others, including Hitler's and Castro's, as falling short of the classic requirements.

The Sorokin classification still seems to me useful and one which we can apply with profit to the contemporary situation in the United States.

It was characteristic of the Russian Revolution (although most of this has long since been lost) that in its early stages the revolutionaries believed they had not only overthrown the Czar but also the whole social and philosophical system that went with him. They believed that they were embarked upon the task of creating a new social order, in fact, these were almost literally Lenin's first words ("We will now proceed to construct the socialist order") in addressing the Soviet after the successful overthrow of November 7, 1917.

In this process, of course, the Russian revolutionaries did not confine themselves merely to economic questions. The whole issue of the relationship of man to man and man to woman was involved. One of the primary objectives of the Bolsheviks was the liberation of women from the tyranny of the czarist social system and an end to the exploitation of women, as they saw it, by a profoundly patriarchal Russian society. This had been an objective long in the making. The whole of nineteenth-century liberal Russia had been engaged with the issue at one time or another. Tolstoy's *Anna Karenina* was perhaps the most powerful single blow struck against the patriarchal structure of laws and mores which enmeshed Russian womanhood. Now, with the new Bolshevik order woman was no longer to be a chattel slave of man, a sex object, a vehicle for the propagation of the race, an inferior creature with few or no legal rights, powerless to extricate herself from male servitude, unable to obtain a divorce, forbidden to seek love where she found it, condemned to the "double standard," discriminated against in legal rights, educational opportunities, employment, freedom of movement, property rights, and in many ways still a psychological residual of the medieval *terem,* the Russified harem system which still had not vanished from provincial and backward urban society and which confined women, in theory, to the home—the Russian equivalent of *kirche, küche, und kinder.*

The Russian revolutionaries counterposed to this their own doctrines of freedom, equality, and liberty. They had long practiced sexual equality among themselves. Relationships between men and women revolutionaries were whatever the men and women desired. Some married, some did not. They respected each other's lives and feelings and tried their best to live on idealistically equal terms, according to the prospectus of Chernyshevsky's famous novel *What Is to Be Done?* Now, they set about to spread their ideas to all of Russian society. Marriage, the formal legal contract, was out. The church wedding, along with everything pertaining to religion, was out. Property rights in marriage were out. You could "register" your marriage or not, as you desired. Each form was equally respected. Divorce was free and easy. A postcard did it. Flaming passion and frequent shifts in love and lovers were characteristic of some vibrant revolutionaries, both male and female, notably Alexandra Kollontai (but she was only a symbol—her example was by no means unusual). Romantic, melodramatic love had always been a Russian tradition. This did not change now. Free love was flaunted by poets and revolutionary orators. Birth control, abortion, the end of the family, the end of subordination of one sex to the other was preached and practiced. (But contrary to the favorite Hearst myth women were never "communized.") So far as costumes and art were concerned—the old went out the window. New "proletarian" styles were the vogue—leather "revolutionary" jackets, long hair for men, short hair for women. The Western cigarette replaced the long-stemmed Russian *papirossi*. Traditional Russian puritanism in art (in real life Russians were far from puritanical—nude mixed bathing was conventional; so was the bold, passionate, male-choosing female living her life in defiance of convention and her counterpart the robust free-loving male)—whatever smacked of the past went out the window, and wild experimentation set in. Whatever had been done was thrown down; whatever had not was glorified.

I mention this because the cultural component of the Russian Revolution was pervasive, just as, of course, was the cultural component of the French Revolution. It was the lack of this overturn of conventional mores, I believe, which compelled Pitirim Sorokin to put the American Revolution to one side, in a class by itself.

It is interesting and not without pertinence that Lenin did not care much for this radical change in Russian custom. In fact, in a famous letter to Alexandra Kollontai he harshly rebuked her and laid down the edict that "love is not just a glass of water" (which is the way she described it). He was a very conventional button-down-collar type himself, although he did have his own inamorata for years, living in a classic menáge à trois with Inessa Armand and his wife. With Lenin's death and the emergence of Stalin, Russia steered back to the stiffest, most straitlaced conventionality, not an unusual revolutionary pattern, and "rights for women" quickly degenerated. Equality not infrequently was typified by the equal right of women to engage in back-breaking street labor, ditch-digging or freight-loading. One thing survived: International Women's Day, when to this day every woman in Russia is given a present by her nearest men. Very good for business, that.

What is pertinent to our contemporary America is the close connection between the revolution in sex and mores and the revolution in politics. The two went hand in hand in Russia, in France, in China, and long before that in another way in Cromwell's England. Thus it is right to perceive the revolution in American mores in a political context. Women's Lib has impeccable political roots. One might, in fact, say that political challenge has spread in the United States, in a sense, from one repressed and undervalued group to another—blacks, young people, Indians, Mexicans, homosexuals, lower-middle-class whites, women—not to mention the Roman Catholic orders. A case can be clearly made that each of these elements in our society is deprived by law and by custom of rights fully exercised by others.

No one needs me to discover for them that a revolution in sex attitudes and mores, in social customs as well as costumes, is far advanced in the United States. It has moved at such a pace that we have, within a period of three or four years, removed literally every barrier to sexual censorship of the printed word. So many handbooks and specialized popular guides to sex conduct, sex habits, sex variations, aberrations, and kinky hangups are being published that they overflow the shelves of conventional, square bookstores, not to mention the creepy salons of 42nd Street. Every four-letter word of the Anglo-Saxon vernacular has appeared not only in the novels of Henry Miller, Norman Mailer, and Philip Roth but in mass circulation magazines and newspapers, with the notable exception of *The New York Times*. In the short exegesis of sexual-execretory terms, only *fart* seems to lag in mass usage. Every kind of photographic representation of human copulatory possibility has been presented in popular "porno" publications, freely sold in almost every city. American-produced "blue" movies differing only in minor detail from the classic stag films of the Elks Club smoker are shown generally and often conventionally reviewed and compared by serious publications. Yale and other universities have run festivals of quasi-porno films and foreign producers of sex films are by way of being put out of business by the more bold American entrepreneurs. The manufacture, advertisement, and sale, over the counter or by mail order, of sex stimulators, simulators, Spanish fly, and other pseudoaphrodisiacs, apparati for every possible kink, are booming. Classic conventions affecting bodily display have wilted under the impact of the see-through dress, the no-bra look, the invisible miniskirt, the halterless bikini, the ritual mixed nude bathing of every youth gathering, political or musical.

A scant three years ago *Hair*, with its plastic nudity, its Dionysian ensembles, symbolized the bold, the daring, the leading edge of the far-out of Off-Broadway. Long since *Hair* has become the contemporary *Abie's Irish Rose*—the must show for every visiting tourist to New York (although, of course, resident and road companies are everywhere from Los Angeles to Paris, France). A couple of years later *Oh! Calcutta* burst on the scene amid dire warnings that the outer limits of the sex barrier were to be publicly penetrated. But the heavens failed to fall—only Kenneth Tynan's reputation in a drumfire of critical abuse for *Calcutta's* banality. It in turn became the conventioneers' delight and, busily raking in the money, retreated into the backdrop of the New York scene, only to emerge occasionally in the provincial headlines.

Critics wondered audibly where the theater could go and answering their own question ruminated on the possibility and feasibility of public sexual exhibitions disguised as drama. It seemed the only gambit left. Even this was hardly likely to raise temperatures jaded by the casual carnality of Times Square, with its bizzarre cornucopia of strolling male and female prostitutes, black, white, yellow, and mixed, whispering or shouting "Buy Me" or "Body for Sale", the serried ranks of porno shops with their genitalia-spattered array of trendy photo albums and 3-D, sound-tracked peepshows; the topless and bottomless bars and the blazing sex movie halls—some for homos (Gay Day, Male Nudes, Stud Affair), some for heteros (Naked Temptress, Los Angeles Stewardesses, Sex—Uninhibited Sex), some for lesbians (The Redliners, The Promiscuous Sex), some for queeros (The Filthy Five, Masha the Promiscuous Housewife), some for the general sidewalk trade (Fear of Love, XYZ's of Love, the ABC's of Sex). There was something for everyone in Times Square and its counterparts across the country but the proprietors of the sex shops unanimously complained that business was lousy. Not even the appearance of pseudo-sex exhibitions in the guise of "plays" in storefront establishments helped much.

The transformation in American conventions rivals those attained in the great movements of the past. Indeed, they far exceed those of the jazz age upheaval of the '20s; the "mauve" revolt of the '90s, and even the sans-culottes of the French Revolution and the sexual liberties of the early Bolsheviks.

Never in the history of the United States has anything like this been seen.

The sweep of the movement affects not only public exhibitory phases of sex conduct—casual intercourse in the open in daylight in public parks, for example, instead of the stealthy passion pits, drive-in movies, lovers lanes, and parked cars—it has moved into the primary areas of marriage ceremony, of childbirth rituals, of procreation customs.

The free-form wedding has spread from one end of the country to the other. Young people vie in imagination to invent new versions. They are marrying in pasture fields and beside the sea, in medieval costumes and full nudity, in slum jungles and pot pads. They compose ceremonies of Ginsberg poetry and Zen chants, of self-written pledges and verses from Keats, of biblical excerpts and rock choruses. In these serene and simple or wild and pulsating ceremonials today's American generation celebrates a new social compact—a compact against tradition, against form without substance, against stereotypes, against words without meaning, against rote, *for* feeling, *for* sensitivity, *for* a bright new world of men and women, *for* love, *for* community.

There is, it seems quite clear, more revolutionary substance in the free-form wedding than Marx could ever pack into his Manifesto, because the new marriage is a pledge of two free beings to each other, to society, and to the world that their life will be based on truth and not on hypocrisy. It cuts to the heart of the social order in a personal and living fashion that is far beyond the eloquence of any dialectic.

There is in the new weddings neither the cant of ecclesiastic ritual nor the cliché of the "Socialist wedding palace," each with its pitiable pretense and cardboard sentiment. Many have abandoned the whole marriage concept except for convenience if they decide to raise children. The menáge à deux in cities like New York, San Francisco, and Los Angeles has moved easily and swiftly from the clandestine to the casual.

But this is only a part albeit perhaps the centerpiece of the revolution in human relations which the young are bringing into three-car suburbia, country-club matriarchy, and executive-suite patriarchy. Thus, there is the whole syndrome of "touch and feel," the Esalen Institute approach in which men and women

strive to shed the masks which conceal and protect their personality and come back to the warmth of bodies and the purity
of emotion by touching, by feeling, by letting their anger, hate,
despair, envy, anguish, and love well out of the plastic molds
in which they have been encapsuled.

Touch me, they say, and with this simple cry protest the
whole technification of the age—the imposition upon man of a
substitute world in which all satisfactions are synthetic—from
food to music, from sex to death.

Revolt against the surrogate nature of American life has
spurred movements for natural childbirth, for the husband to
stand beside his wife during childbirth, of breast nursing (despite
the fact that the American mother's breast gives milk so con-
taminated by DDT that it could not pass interstate inspection).
And now is arising a move to end the puppetry and commercialization of death—the confinement of the dying to anesthetically
removed cells, far from the living, and their burial to the accom-
paniment of wall-to-wall carpet, music, stainless coffins, and
perpetual oratory. For, say the critics, death is as common as
life. Life must end in death. Why, then, create a society in which
Death has no presence, in which we pretend it does not exist.
Why should not Death be the final act in the Human Drama
instead of being concealed behind a hospital sheet far from the
living, and far from the young? Why should not the Scene be
played as it was in Victorian and pre-Victorian times—as the
natural culmination of human existence? Many medical scholars
feel that we have radically damaged the quality of existence by
sweeping Death under the carpet. Concerned with the leaching
out of human values and the cosmetic rhetoric employed to wall-
paper death from the living and the dying they have founded a
new discipline called "thanatology" to try to reintegrate death
with life, to bring an end to customized expressions like "passing
away," to break the muted stereophonic image of perpetual

life, to bring grief and sorrow and sadness and love back into the climax which crowns every life, to make real the fact that man is mortal, that neither electronics nor Helena Rubinstein have written a new ending to the age-old saga.

So goes the new reasoning. How to match it with the confinement of the aged into "Golden Shores" communities and the rapacious promotional death barracks of the real-estate fraternity has not yet been resolved. But the logical step would be the resurrection of the extended family—already foreshadowed in the spread of the cult-tribe and the pseudofamily, the commune, the grouping of individuals in living centers and communities in which all participate in one another's lives, the permutation of sexual combinations, the multiplication of surrogate fathers, surrogate children.

Underlying the new ease, permissiveness, casualness, openness of the young toward the rigid mores-bound world of sex lies not only philosophy but technology. It is no accident that the forward thrust into new and liberated sexual relationships was given by the Pill. Once woman possessed a mechanism which, for practical purposes, made her the equal of man in determining the procreative results of sex, she rapidly moved to attitudes and relations of true equality. The Pill, regardless of the controversy over the possible ultimate side effects, gives women genuine Liberation, which no other method of procreational control had offered.

Whether the Pill has increased sexual activity can be argued. But it gives women a security and a confidence which they did not previously possess. So far as middle-class parents are concerned it dissolved sex conventions more rapidly than any decree from on high and in the process demonstrated that the virginity myths were, as sociologists had long argued, based primarily on ancient tribal taboos to maintain the purity of the line, to prevent random crossbreeding. Middle-class mothers might still inveigh against their daughters staying out too late. But they didn't worry so much about the results because they made certain that the girls were equipped with the Pill. The daughters might not indulge more frequently in sex. But they could shed fear, guilt, and anxiety. They were able to enjoy it as much as the boys.

If there still are residual barriers so far as the Catholic church is concerned, it is only too apparent in most American dioceses that regardless of equivocation in Rome the trend of the times, in Catholic homes as well as non-Catholic, is simply to accept the control of births and all that it implies.

Nor did it end with the Pill. The introduction of the Pill and its universal adoption and use made the next giant step easy and inevitable. I mean, of course, the legalization of abortion. This had stood like a Chinese wall around women, the wall which so many of them had seemingly supported, although the ban on abortion could by no means work to woman's good. Suddenly, as though it had arisen out of nowhere, came the move to legalize abortion. Was this a social revolution? There can be no question about it. For the abortion statutes went to the very heart of social attitudes and of prejudice concerning human relations and of life itself. It touched the most ancient of human philosophies. Yet, within a single year the enormous palisaded legal fortress which had driven American women into the hands of the ignorant midwife or the protected, Mafia-controlled, illicit practitioner in his grubby hideaway in one of the cesspool communities of Jersey—to pay $700 for an operation far simpler than pulling a tooth, to invest $1,000 in a round-trip journey to Puerto Rico or Japan for a service which a competent practitioner could perform in 20 minutes—was swept into the discard. And the end is not yet. Women's Lib has demanded free on-demand abortion and it is likely they will win this along with child day-care centers and equal employment and educational opportunity.

Yes. I think Pitirim Sorokin would have classed what is happening in the United States as a true revolution, a profound revolution, one which radically modifies the relations between men and women, their attitudes not only toward each other but toward the totality and meaning of life.

This is what the Jerry Rubins of the world (and the tired, dialectic-numbed Marxists) mean when they talk about a life-style revolution. They mean a genuine change in the way people feel toward one another and toward their life. They mean a new freedom in how people act as well as think, in how they dress and how they make love, a freedom to do their own thing, and, most important of all, respect for the freedom of others to do their own thing.

This, I submit, is not easy to take for those who are rigid in their ways, those who feel that God ordained that every man should have his hair cut once a month to a length of about three and a half inches long, that every woman should wear a comfortable and modest brassiere, that marriages are made in heaven and ceremonialized in church, that woman's place is in the home (or working as a clerk or stenographer), that it is blasphemy to interfere with natural reproduction, and that the Tijuana Brass are as far out as the Founding Fathers intended that music should go.

Can the country undergo a social-cultural revolution without a politicio-economic one as well?

I don't know and I don't think even Charles Reich can be sure. But there is in the air something as profound as, say, the Reformation or the Renaissance—something which cuts across the whole swath of human conduct. What is happening in the United States, here and now, touches life more deeply than the Cultural Revolution of Chairman Mao or the westernization of Japan—two other cataclysmic events of this century.

Bear this in mind. These cultural changes are not confined to

the United States. In many ways their inceptions has come from
other lands, far distant—European, Asian, and African. If you
examine the intimate cultural interchange which now links the
world (about which I have insisted in previous chapters), then
you must conclude that we are witnessing radical changes in
social-cultural structure not only in the United States but in
much of the world. Because, as I hope to demonstrate in the next
chapter, man, American man, is not only behaving in new ways
and in new patterns, he is changing basically in what he thinks
and believes.

CHAPTER 14

The Cross and the Lotus

Four years ago I was lunching with a quiet, merry-eyed Sister, dean of studies at a midwestern Catholic school for girls. We were talking about conditions in Latin America and the role of the priesthood in attempting to bring about social reform. The sister spent her summers in Latin America, working with the peasants.

"Of course," she said, "the only hope of change is revolution. The society and government is completely corrupt. Almost all the young priests know this and work for it."

But what of the church, what of the hierarchy? I asked.

"Oh," she said, "I pray every night for the death of the old bishop. No. You needn't be shocked. He is nearly eighty. He has led a good life. Now it is time that the younger men took over. It is the only way."

I looked out across the middle western countryside, drowsing in the warm October sun, and let the sister's words sink in. She was as gentle and intelligent as any woman I have ever met, yet she was praying for the death of an old bishop so that the cause of revolution in one of the Latin countries might move forward under the leadership of the Roman church.

It was more of a shock than it might be today. For today we live in an era in which Catholic priests, frequently backed by their superiors, support the cause of revolution in more than one Latin country. We live in an era in which priests and nuns have stood in the forefront of struggle in the United States for integration, for equality of blacks and whites; in which they have opened their churches and their schools to blacks and whites; in which they have led marches for peace and against the war in Vietnam; in which they run for office, win places in Congress and in local government; in which the brothers Berrigan have led civil disobedience to the draft laws and even gone underground in defiance of the U.S. government; in which the Roman church has supported progressive and radical causes in Western Europe; in which priests and bishops, mothers superior and cardinals have publicly opposed the church's ban on birth control and have fought for the end of celibacy and for a married priesthood.

There are those who attribute all this to Pope John. But, of course, this is a simplification. The changes in the church have long been fermenting. They have come to the surface with dramatic speed and explosive effect because the period of maturation has been so long and because the men and women of the church are, and always have been, permeated with deep idealism, with a purity of conscience, with a nobility which, although sometimes constrained or distorted by a regressive or power-conscious hierarchy, swiftly and irresistibly came to the surface once conditions were ripe.

Careless observers sometimes say that the church is on the decline and that God is dead. But, surely, only the blind and the deaf could be ignorant of the profound religiosity of the present day.

Walk down Fifth Avenue and watch the incongruous but irresistible progress of a band of Buddhists. They wear the salmon or saffron robes of Asia. Their heads are shaven. They ring the brass bells of the Asian mendicant. But look again: these are young Americans, fresh-faced, smiling, speaking with patience and kindness to curious and rude passersby.

Visit the great Zen temple in Kyoto and note those who sit in silence contemplating the garden of sand and rocks. There are more Americans than Japanese.

There were snickering smirks when Allen Ginsberg chanted the Om at the trial of the Chicago Seven, but its resonance brought a sudden solemnity into an inherently comic confrontation.

What is it that is sought by those who use hallucinogens? Why do young people gather for quiet reverie amid Oriental symbols, listening to the chant of Hindu poets, the words of the gurus, the distant jangle of the bronze bells? What takes them on pilgrimages of thousands of miles to the dusty temple steps of Katmandu or Bangkok? Is it mere search for sensation? Escape from a world, from a life which they reject? In part, perhaps, yes. Ever since man began to seek a God he has begun by moving away from here and now into the past and future. To refuse the banality of the present is the first step toward Godhood.

What is important to us is that life in the latter third of the twentieth century has stirred the young in countless, endless numbers to seek for a faith, a faith of their own, to seek for a God or a meaning in life. Only those hopelessly addicted to the cult of the commonplace, to the conventional Sunday creed, be it Catholic or Baptist, can fail to recognize that a new and powerful religiosity has sprung out of the depths of human beings who are alive to the necessity of man's finding a key to himself and who have turned their backs on the old and the trite not because they are irreligious, godless, or atheistic but precisely because they are religious and have discovered in the churches of their parents' choice that there reigns convention, not faith, cult not truth.

But this only touches the surface of what must be the most vibrant and vital religious milieu since Martin Luther hammered his ninety-five theses to the great doors of the Cathedral of Wittenberg in 1517. Out of the ranks of harassed, harried, and convention-dulled Protestantry has emerged a corps of idealistic, truth-seeking, sacrificial leaders. They have come from a dozen sects to take their places at the head of every morally inspired movement which has swept America in the past decade. They have marched more miles than the Jews in their wanderings in the Wilderness—to Selma, to Birmingham, to the cotton delta of Mississippi, to Washington and to Washington again, to Chicago, to the city halls, the city squares, the village greens, the civic centers of all America. They have joined their ecumenical brothers, the Jews, in filling the ranks of peace movements and civil rights movements, of integration movements and antiwar movements. They have gone from door to door to solicit funds and to solicit votes. They have provided succor and refuge for the hunted and the oppressed. They have given life and blood and meaning to the words of their dogmas.

Some may say and some may believe that this is an age of materialism. I do not. I believe we live in an age of antimaterialism on a massive scale and that the commitment of so many in the churches, Protestant and Catholic, and in the synagogues, Reformed and Orthodox, is evidence of this. Just as the evidence is to be found in the conduct of the young, what they are really doing, not some careless distortion, some angry impression. At *The New York Times* Symposium on the Decades Walter Kerr and Clive Barnes commented on the deep religiosity of the young people in the universities and of their search for a new kind of religion since so many had abandoned the conventions of the past.

"Up until the present generation people regularly went to church, regularly went to temple," Barnes said, but now they do not. Thus, young people at the theater are "having mystic experiences rather like going to a religious service."

"When you get people without the togetherness that religion gives them they are going to search in other fields," he added. Kerr felt that young people saw their experiences in the theater, particularly the free-form experimental theater, as basically spiritual or religious rather than aesthetic.

The search for belief has moved in so many directions that, looking at it from afar, one is left in a whirl. There is the superstitious kind of mysticism, flourishing under the signs of the zodiac, the belief in the magical qualities of the "Age of Aquarius," the return to Tarot and astrology, the genuine and touching but sometimes frightening and profoundly disturbed experimentation with witchcraft, closely linked to drug cults and drug culture, the belief in witches and warlocks, in supernatural sight, vision, powers, in the evil eye, in the ability to see in, though, around, and past the future, a theory and tendency elaborated by Harvey Cox in *The Feast of Fools.*

Cox finds in all of this, in part, a massive put-on, a monumental turn-off from mechanistic-materialistic, computer-ordained society. And, no doubt, it is this in part. (Example: computerized horoscopes at Grand Central stalls.) But basically it is, of course, an important evidence of the tenacious human search for a meaning to existence, for rosy tints or distant visions which will soften the impossibly harsh, ax-blunt outlines of life in the nonhuman context which it has achieved in the United States and to a lesser extent the other "advanced" countries of the West. And it is a very serious search, indeed, for in Cox's words, "Christ was part yippie and part revolutionary and part something else."

It is no accident that this movement finds little reflection in the new societies of Africa or Asia, including China. For these are lands just standing on the edge of materialism, the steam engine, the gasoline combustion device, not to mention the computer and the atom. Nor should we be surprised to find that a search for lost nationalism, not mysticism, is more likely to prevail among black activists.

It is not stretching the image very much to connect the search for spirit and spirituality, for significance and mystery, to the tidal wave of the Earth movement. I could call this movement Conservation, Environment—almost anything. But I think "Earth" is the best word because this is an atavistic crusade bearing little relationship to the middle-aged orientation of the Save-the-Birds, Spare-the-Tree campaigns of the past. This is a profound, inner-oriented, passionate, instinctual drive which seeks, it seems to me, to preserve and recapture the earth as man's habitat—his habitat, complete with the natural life which so long was his environment. It is this, I believe, that has given the movement its tidal flow, which has swept up the young on their bicycles and the old with their yearning for the age of horses, which produces the boom in health foods (a mystique in itself), raw fabrics, handicrafts, non-polluted, nontainted with the evils of the twentieth century. It is this which sends the young commune dwellers into the Vermont forests to grub out a living on a small corn patch and a back-breaking sugar grove of maple trees and to bake their own bread.

We face the clear and present danger of the final and destructive exhaustion of the earth, which stimulates our Darwinian survival urge. But this comes through to us as an almost compulsive religioisity. We are violent in our determination to purge the rivers and lakes of the detergents and mercury which have turned them into cesspools; we are revolutionary in our assault on power-company predators of the waters and the mountains; we jab and twist at the storied redoubts of the concrete-and-highway monopolists; we assault the oil companies savagely, our guilt at boiling point, no doubt, for our shameless use of leaded elements and octanes. We walk beside the cluttered sea and weep.

There is no doubt that a cult of nature, a religion of the earth, is in the making—and the earth and nature is the oldest worship known to man. It is a cult of new priests, of Paul Ehrlich, the Sierra Club, and zero population growth. It rages against the junk car, the disposable bottle, packaged detergents, chemical fertilizers, and the sheer bulk of *The New York Times.*

You may not see an immediate connection between the young people of Cambridge who have pledged themselves not to use the gasoline combustion engine and the young Zen acolytes begging on Fifth Avenue, between the resolute warrior-lawyers who fight Storm King and the Berrigan brothers, between beautiful girls pledged to bear no more children and the SDS. But I see a close and intimate connection. I see a society searching for basics, a society which has turned not against the substance of its truth but against the forms in which that truth has been containerized, a society which is at one and the same time seeking and creating a new faith and a new mystique.

This is peculiarly American—American middle class and upper income. You will range the world and find few in Asia who worry about Mother Nature. You will find no one in Africa who inveighs against DDT. DDT is giving many an African nation a first chance at lowering the hideous death toll of mosquito- and larvae-borne disease. It has taken half a dozen years of tough fighting by a handful of Russian conservationists to get their government grudgingly to move against the despoliation of Lake Baikal, one of the world's wonders. It has taken the decline of the caviar industry to arouse Moscow to the near-death of the polluted Volga.

Only when we benefit luxuriously from a bountiful earth can we afford the time and emotion to see how we have ravaged her. Indeed, it is only in the most recent years that scientists and social thinkers have begun to challenge the idea which is central to Judeo-Christian doctrine—namely, that the earth is the paradise which God placed at man's beck and call, to be used to enrich him, to comfort him, to clothe him, to feed him, to do with as he pleases.

The idea of the earth as Eden, a treasure chest, a pool of infinite riches to be savored, to be used, to put to man's employment as he pleases and how he pleases has been with us as long as the myth of Adam and Eve—so long that we have taken for granted that when we want gold we dredge the streams and burrow under the mountains, when we want oil we penetrate the earth's crust and pump to our heart's desire, when we want wheat we tear off the cover of trees and grass and sow our seeds, devil take the hindmost and wind take the topsoil, when we want food we shoot the birds and plunder the fishes, when we want clothing we skin the hides from gentle animals. We are the kings, the earth is our domain, and all that lives, all that exists, is subject to our command.

No other faith, no other philosophy, views the earth in this light—not Buddhism, not Confucianism, not Hinduism. Each sees man as the child of earth, as the inheritor, as the protector, as the beneficiary of an enormous trust. The philosophical difference is critical.

For now, as we ponder the ruin which we have wrought of earth, we begin to question the fundamentals of our philosophy.

It is in this process that for the first time, I think, since the Reformation we have begun to look anew and askance at the basic premises of our life. We have begun under the leadership of our young people to seek new meanings beyond the dollar, beyond the depletion allowance, beyond the production plan, beyond the concept that more is better and that progress means bigger and bigger. We have found that we want for life a genuine significance, that we wish to discard verbiage and find meaning, that we are not czars unbound by rules but mortal men who need one another and a warm and lively earth in which to live—it is all this which is giving to our age its special connotation. We are travelers on Planet Earth. We have for the first time visited the Moon. We are proud and aware of our technical competence. We can do anything—or almost anything. But suddenly we have looked at ourselves and our fruits and have begun to ask, Is this our creation? Is this what we wish? Are these the ends we seek?

Is Jersey City, the Tokyo slums, Russia's labor camps, the heroin factories of Naples, the corpse-cluttered streets of Calcutta, the robot-life of Shanghai, the sullen racism of London—is this the goal of modern man? Is this our best, our finest?

And no one gives the answer Yes. Each says No. Each turns against the reality which we have created and each in his own way and by his own means looks for something more true—possibly in the uncapturable nostalgia of the past, possibly in the haze of superstition, possibly in the giving of self without barrier to the ennoblement of brothers, sisters, comrades. But no one answers Yes. No one says, Yes—this is what man wants—the dead animals, the barren skies, the lowering yellow fog, the burning dumps, the fetid streets, the angry brawling crowds, the crunch of the policeman's club, the thin whine of the Guardsman's bullet, the roar of the dynamite bomb, the glazed eyes of the bloody dead. No one says Yes to this. All say No.

CHAPTER 15

A Long Way from Little Rock

I happened to be traveling in Eastern Europe at the time of Little Rock. It was a depressing place—Albania, a Lilliput Stalinist survival; Bulgaria, no U.S. diplomatic relations; Rumania, not yet Peck's Bad Boy of Communism; Hungary, a year after Budapest and still in shock; Czechoslovakia, frozen and dull; Poland, sullen and restless.

Travel in Eastern Europe was lonely, difficult, disheartening. Little Rock made it more so. In every country, on every hand, from everyone I got Little Rock. It was hurled at me by Communist party secretaries, ground in by Communist editors, sadly mentioned by sympathetic writers. How could it be? How could America, the most advanced country in the world, the symbol of truth, justice, equality, the model toward which all aspired, the nation whose streets were paved with gold, the country where every uncle in Eastern Europe had made his fortune, how could this blessed land let Little Rock happen? That was as mildly as it was put. Tough-mouthed party hacks twisted the dagger deeper and deeper. Little Rock was the answer to why Albania lived on the verge of starvation, why Bulgaria had no liberties. It explained Rumania's reluctance to move away from the Moscow party line and the deep cynicism of the boys and girls in the Budapest cafés. Things might be bad in Prague but *Rude Pravo* made them seem better by devoting a page to Little Rock. Of course, it was an old, old Communist device. There was not one American tourist in Russia during the 1930s who, complaining about service at the Metropole Hotel, did not get the rejoinder "What about the Scottsboro case?"

But Little Rock was not a case of the 1930s. In 1957 it was here and now and it followed me through the Balkans like a mangy dog. I never escaped it, but I did find a way of responding. I accepted Little Rock as a scandal. But I invited my Communist critics to look at the event in context. It had not occurred in isolation. It was not a random act of racism. It happened because for the first time a great nation was attempting to do what had never been done before in human history—it was attempting to lay the foundation for a multiracial society in which legal discrimination, government prejudice, social inequity, deliberate deprivation, would be ended and for the first time Americans of all colors would live together under our stated principle that "all men are created free and equal." This, I submitted, was a noble and epochal undertaking. No feeling, no prejudice, no hatred known to man ran deeper than that of race. Never had a society existed which was truly color blind. Now in the twentieth century the United States, slowly, painfully, belatedly, was moving to accomplish that goal. Thousands of lives had been sacrificed to race bigotry. I was certain that the toll would be considerable in the future. The path was not going to be smooth. One did not wipe out ancient impacted feelings without agony. But, I said, we are on the way. Little Rock is one battle in the long campaign. What is important is not that we have lost a skirmish or suffered casualties. What is important is that we are on the way to something which mankind has never achieved before. And we are going to do it.

I made that speech in Sofia, in Bucharest, in Budapest, in Prague, and Warsaw. I was given no chance to make it in Tirana. But I did try it out on the poor young man who had been designated to act as my guide-bodyguard-personal spy. I don't know what he thought of it. His instructions, obviously, were never to agree with anything I said. But in the other Balkan countries my remarks evoked a serious, thoughtful response. Problems of color are not common in the Balkans. But problems of race and tribe and religion and nationality are. There was not a Bulgarian, a Rumanian, a Hungarian, or a Pole who did not solemnly nod his head and agree that no prejudices were more difficult to change than those involving race.

Of course, that is what few of us in the United States stop to consider. The race question has not been resolved in any country—not in ancient times, not in medieval times. Not today. Not under Buddhism, not under Catholicism. Not in Western Europe, and certainly not in any of the 57 varieties of communism which now spatter the world.

Race prejudice is deeply ingrained in Russia, although you will find few members of the Soviet intelligentsia who admit this. But try a conversation on the subject of China and watch the hatred and fear of the yellow races—the Mongols and the Chinese —come bubbling to the surface. Russia was invaded 700 years ago by the Mongols, who kept the country in subjection for nearly 300 years. The mark is indelible. Nothing in Russian Orthodoxy or Marxist communism has blurred it. In theory, of course, Soviet Russia has wiped out all trace of racial chauvinism. But this did not keep Moscow University students from behaving like hard hats when black Africans began to appear in considerable numbers. The frictions grew so intense Moscow set up a segregated university and segregated dormitories for the blacks. Russia has never had a black population except for a few slaves brought in during the time of Peter the Great and a tiny black tribe in the remote Caucasus numbering less than 200 persons. During Depression days several hundred American Negroes emigrated to Russia and lived a feted life until World War II. They were great curiosities and won enormous affection because everyone knew about slavery and lynching and the Scottsboro boys. (All Russian children read *Uncle Tom's Cabin* and it is still a major attraction at the Moscow Children's Theater.) But the war changed everything. The Russians had no time or inclination to bother with Negroes in their struggle against Hitler. The American Negroes barely survived the war and postwar years. They lost their jobs, even their living places. Some had no ration cards during the grim wartime years.

There is little reservoir of sympathy toward American blacks in today's Russia. As one young Russian put it in 1970, "You should know that we have come to understand something about the blacks ourselves. We have had them in the university in Moscow. Very unpleasant. You won't find much sympathy in Russia for the Black Panthers and the black movement in the United States."

The same type of situation prevails in China. No people, not even the Russians, have a deeper, longer tradition of racial chauvinism than the Chinese. The Chinese traditionally did not regard any people but themselves, that is, the Han peoples, as human. All others were some kind of white monsters. When the Chinese called Europeans "barbarians" this was what they had in mind. It is true that Mao Tse-tung now rules rather than the Dowager Empress. But basic Chinese racial attitudes have not changed. Every minority people around China's periphery complains of Han chauvinism—the Uighurs, the Kazaks, the Mongols. Robert Williams, the black radical, who lived in Peking for several years, returned to the United States in relief. He found it difficult to establish a meaningful relationship with the Chinese. Stokeley Carmichael had a rather similar experience in Hanoi.

Eldridge Cleaver has based himself in Algiers, which may provide a more compatible environment.

What is important is not the individual experience of black leaders in Communist countries. What is important is the simple fact that no Communist regime has ended race prejudice or race discrimination. Nowhere but in the United States has there been mounted against race a vast soul-rending effort—mass political agitation, radical confrontation, countrywide education, governmental police powers, courts and legal mechanisms, economic pressures and contrivances, religious and moral crusades—the full panoply of mechanisms at the command of society.

To be sure, progress has been slow, much too slow, too back-sliding, too painful, too tragic, too two-steps-forward, one-step-backward, too costly, too disruptive, too bloody, too frustrating, too polarizing. But progress there has been. Under an indecisive Eisenhower, an energetic Kennedy, an impulsive Johnson, and a cautious Nixon the movement has not halted.

I was in the South in 1960 when the sit-ins were starting. I felt the excitement, the thrill, when half a dozen black youngsters sauntered into a Woolworth's in Nashville and sat down at the soda fountain. What a simple form the revolutionary act sometimes takes. To sit on a lunch stool and order a ham sandwich. And a Coke. But revolutionary it was. As revolutionary as the clenched fist and the "Right on!" of the Black Panther. It took as much courage, or more. For it had never been done before. Not one of the youngsters from Fisk or Vanderbilt really knew what would happen. The cops were just as big. The concept of the "uppity nigger" was fresher, clearer, more real, in 1960 than in 1970.

I traveled the southern circuit that year—Orangeburg, S.C., Charlotte and Raleigh, Baton Rouge, New Orleans, Montgomery, and, of course, Birmingham. Wherever I went I saw black people, mostly young, doing revolutionary things. Sometimes young whites joined them, sometimes not. They sat down at five-and-dime lunch counters and drugstore soda fountains. They sat in the front seats of buses. They used "white only" waiting rooms in railroad stations and airports. They used "white only" toilets and "white only" drinking fountains. Some even dared to appear at swimming pools and beaches and golf courses. No signs there. But everyone knew who was allowed and who wasn't. These were revolutionary acts. Every day the face of the South was changing. Everyone south of the Mason-Dixon line understood this and you could feel the tension thicken. Everyone knew that the revolution meant violence. The established order would not stand for this. It would fight back and it had the guns, it had the muscle, it had the bully squads, the goons, the hate, and the will. It was just a matter of when and where. I ventured the guess that Birmingham would blow up. I could smell the sputter of the powder train. Birmingham's Bull Connor and his fellow city officials sued *The Times* and myself for several million dollars. Gross libel, they said. Everything was fine in Birmingham. Just hunky-dory. But, tragically and inevitably, Birmingham did blow up. Libel suit or no. Blacks died. Blood was shed. Dynamite exploded. Guns chattered.

When it was over, of course, the blacks won and Bull lost, even in the courts, even to *The Times.*

Ten years. Not long in the endless stream of human history. But a lifetime for those who have waited half a dozen generations for justice, for equality, for freedom. How far is it from Octavius Roy Cohn's Catfish Row to Adam Clayton Powell's Baptist church in Harlem? Perhaps not so far. Perhaps hardly any distance at all. But Catfish Row was moving into history while Powell continued into the present. I listened to Powell preach the funeral oration for W. C. Handy, the "father of the blues," and then marched with the multitude through the streets of Harlem in the solemn cortege led by the brass band of the Prince Hall Masonic Temple, playing "The St. Louis Blues." I listened to Adam Clayton Powell cry from the pulpit of the Abyssinian church:

"His personal blues are now finished.
No more the problems of Beale Street.
No more the irritations of Memphis.
No more the vexations of the St. Louis Woman.
No more the cynical Love, Oh, Love, Oh, Careless Love."
I listened to Powell speak. I marched behind the brass band and today I cannot imagine that it ever happened. It belongs to another era in history, to another life. I cannot relate it to Little Rock, to Bull Connor, and certainly not to the world of today. For today and long since the struggle has come to the North. As predicted, as inevitable.

One night I sat in a white-tiled restaurant on 125th Street and listened to a serious, spectacled, soft-spoken, light-skinned black man talking in quiet, dignified tones, analyzing the position of his people, telling of the black male's loss of manhood, of the loss of self-respect of the whole black people, telling of his own single-minded, dedicated determination to win his people back for themselves. This was Malcolm X and I thought as I listened to the thoughtful, almost religious discourse how much he must resemble the Narodniki of Russia's 1870s, and how the black movement was beginning to gather a revolutionary scope, the kind of thing which had swept other basically peasant peoples in the past, and for the first time I made the connection of the blacks as a great peasant class impacted in a twentieth-century technological America.

So it went. The Movement came north. It came north, black and proud and militant, and slammed right up against a power structure and a power apparatus tougher than any Bull Connor ever conceived.

There was the first wave of riots, the first wave of destruction. It started in Harlem over a shooting outside a school not 200 feet from where I lived, a school I hardly knew existed, a quiet, inconspicuous school in a placid middle-class New York East Side neighborhood. It began as these things always begin with a triviality, a janitor's quarrel with rude children. Then blood was spilled and suddenly a black boy lay dying on the sidewalk, a foolish, futile, mindless tragedy of the kind which happens every day in big cities like New York. But that night and the next night Harlem exploded. Then, it spread, city after city, culminating in Watts. That was the first wave. The violence receded but not for long. There was a second wave—Detroit and Cleveland and a dozen others. The tensions in the country rose. The ghettos burned and assassins' bullets took the lives of the leaders, black and white, radical and conservative—Malcolm X, John F. Kennedy, Martin Luther King, George Lincoln Rockwell, Medgar Evers, three civil rights workers in Mississippi, Robert Kennedy, Panthers in one city after another. Violence fed on violence until one day, running for a plane at Newark airport I heard a woman ask her husband, "What's all that smoke?" "Oh," he responded, "they're burning down Newark." And we all hurried on for the plane, not waiting to watch Newark burn, more anxious to get on to our many separate engagements out around the country. Newark was burning. Too bad. That was the day after Martin Luther King was shot.

So the tensions rose. The lines drew sharper. Blacks separated from whites in the "movement." They wanted to fight their own battle, determine their own fate, win their own victories. But with rising strength the radical fringes, black and white, inched closer together as terror matched violence, the police "riot" appeared on the American scene, the anarchists' bombs exploded—first tentatively, then with greater frequency.

Gradually the image of the Black Panthers mounted larger and larger in the ghettos and cast its shadow over the national scene, spreading eastward from Oakland, aided by the blood of martyrs as police guns took Panther lives in what invariably were officially described as shoot-outs, and invariably characterized by surviving Panthers as massacres.

There the struggle stood as the first year of the 1970s played out. The guns were everywhere and in the ghettos a mounting toll of police lives gave anguished testimony to the accuracy of the snipers, once a figment of too vivid police imagination but now a phenomenon brutally and murderously real.

Black-and-white, black-and-white—to many it seemed that Armageddon was at hand, the final reckoning, the show-down and shoot-out in the ghettos, on one hand the armored cars, the grenade-launchers, the flak-jacketed mobile police, on the other the lean and silent black defense forces, mounted in ghetto windows, ghetto roofs, ghetto hideouts.

That was the Doomsday version.

But another scenario was projected improbably from the South, from the dark and bloody soil where blacks and whites had lived in enforced bondage since the beginning of the "peculiar institution." From the South came clear evidence that predictions of doom and gloom should not be too readily credited. Here on the land where blacks so long had suffered and whites, almost unknowingly, had suffered too, began to emerge the pattern of a cultural and racial adjustment which, against all odds, might lead the nation out of the tortured impasse into which it had been driven.

From one southern state after another came new word. Blacks were prospering. Blacks were winning political power. Blacks were making their stand in the South and creating a viable world. White southerners, despite their rambunctious, bumptious, doltish politicians, were finding their own way of living with the present instead of dreaming of the past.

What was happening in the South, or so it seemed, was that those fundamentals which so many had said lay at the root of the trouble—economics, politics, legal rights—had proved just that. Black southerners were winning decent jobs in factories and government installations. Black southerners were voting and electing blacks to office or helping to elect whites. Black southerners were going to court and winning their rights. Blacks and whites, for all

the hubbub, all the ritual Wallaciania, were going to school together. Blacks and whites were carrying guns, a pistol in the
jeans, a shotgun in the pickup. Perhaps that was the difference.
Before only the whites carried guns. Now all did and used them
less. Blacks were moving up through the educational system,
through high school, through college. *And they were staying in
the South.* This was the great breakthrough. No longer were they
piling into the buses, hitching rides on trucks, crowding into
beat-up Chevrolets and Fords and heading for Cleveland, Buffalo,
Hartford, and Newark. They were staying in the South. They
liked it better there. They found the opportunities more reward-
ing. They knew how to get along. Race prejudice, they said, was
less in the South than in the North.

I don't want to sound too optimistic. God knows the South is
no paradise. God knows the fragile and tentative emergence of a
modus vivendi could be zapped by one terrible, devastating act.
But it must be recorded against all the prophecies of the Doomsday men, against those who thought that peace could never come
to the South after Little Rock, after Oxford, Mississippi, after
Selma, after Birmingham—after the whole long bloody roll call of
terrors, that in the summer of 1970 quietly, without civic celebra-
tions, without fanfare, the flowers of hope were as clearly visible
below the Mason-Dixon line, as plain to see as the auguries of
terror and trouble that spread like thin lanes of fire from one
"progressive" northern community to another, nowhere more
visibly, nowhere more portentously than in that great citadel of
progressivism, that symbol and workshop of futurism—California.

Indeed, autumn 1970 was a long, long way from Little Rock.
So far, I fear, that even black militants would have a hard time
recalling what happened at Little Rock (Governor Faubus, President Eisenhower, federal troops, and all that).

It is a long way from Little Rock to guerrilla fighting in the
black ghettos, to intimations that the tactics of Che Guevara were
taking root in the South Side of Chicago and in the placid and

pungent slums of Philadelphia. It was a long way from Little
Rock to the mobilization of national security agencies, the FBI,
the coordinated police facilities of state and city against black
militants, the perception of black militants as a genuine revolutionary force.

But that is the distance we have traveled in fifteen years;
that is the distance in danger and I do not want to minimize it.
But before we permit ourselves to be suffocated by fear or
drowned in horror, let's take another look at Dixie. Perhaps
there is a middle way and perhaps it will be found not in the
ugly asphalt battlegrounds of the North but down in that sad
and sorrowful land of cotton where more than 200 years ago
the trouble all began. Perhaps it is time to go back to what I
said in Sofia, in Bucharest, and in Prague in 1957—we have embarked on a long struggle to attain the impossible, to achieve
what has never been achieved in the history of human society.
We are not going to win the struggle without casualties, victims,
sacrifices, losses, tragedies. No one has done it before. Perhaps,
as many think, it can't be done. But, perhaps, we will confound
the doubting Thomases. It is an impossible dream and perhaps
because of this very impossibility we will make it all come true. I
am not prepared to toss in my hand, to say that the odds are too
long, the chances too small. Looking ahead it may seem that we
have a long way to go (as we do), but looking back to Little
Rock we can see that we have already come much, much further
than most people ever believed was possible.

CHAPTER 16

"My God! We're Losing a Great Country"

The fields are yellow today with goldenrod and white with Queen Anne's lace, and light frost has left the first bright traces of autumn on the mountaintops of the Berkshires. Crows argue in the pasture and apples have reddened in the upland orchard. Summer is passing but the spring's agony has not left the land. It lies in the belly of the country like an ulcer, knotting our spirits with pain. Sniper's bullets fly in the ghettos. Police guns hammer in exchange. Bombs spatter blood on the harvest moon of the drowsy cornlands which for years John McCutcheon's drawings idealized in the *Chicago Tribune*.

Where have we come since that cool May day with its dandelions, its stench of vomit and oozing blood on the campus greens? Where are we now and where are we going? There are

solemn savants who weigh the evidence and proclaim we stand
on the verge of national nervous breakdown. I don't know what
a national nervous breakdown is and I doubt they do. But it
makes for openers at the chic cocktail parties. And there are
the others, the ones who keep talking about the generations, the
differences between the fathers and the sons. Some have read
Turgenev and tell how the America of the 1970s resembles the
Russia of the 1870s. This is an even better gambit. There are
so many points of convergence—the young Narodniki, taking their
crusade to the "dark people," the ignorant Russian peasant
masses, just freed from serfdom, dedicating their lives to these
simple souls who often murdered their benefactors, certain that
the young people were up to some devil's trick. The parallel to
SNCC, to the way the blacks turned against the whites who
carried the word to Mississippi, seems so apt. Then there was
the second phase in Russia when the young idealists, harassed,
battered, and persecuted by the Czar's police, moved on to terror
and sought with bomb and pistol, with desperate conspiracy and
assassination, to kill the Czar and bring down the whole structure of the state, dreaming that thus they could rally the multitude to their cause. For this, too, there seemed a parallel in
the switch to violence in the ghettos and on the campus, the
gun-for-gun tactics of the Panthers, the wild plot-and-counterplot
of the Weathermen, the detonation of explosives at towering
targets from one end of the land to another.

Out of the violence arose an anguish that echoed through the
cities—was this, then, the way it all would end, in a crescendo
of hate, of violent left against terrorist right; of blue power:
the tension-raddled, manic police, unlimbering zap guns and
plastic grenades, unleashing frustrations on any target which
met the eye, in police riots at Isla Vista, Los Angeles, Boston,
Philadelphia; of anarchist terror, equally frustrated, equally
maximalist, striking at random, blowing up buildings, heedless
of who was killed, turning to the sniper's gun and, possibly, kid-

naping and "execution"?

Who could help fearing we had taken the first steps down a dark road from which there was no turning?

In May a student at the New School cried, "My God! We're losing a great country." By autumn there were those who said, "We have lost it. There is no exit. Next stop—civil war in the cities, Hitler in Washington." Among the Cassandras there was easy belief in the oft-denied rumors of concentration camps made ready in the West for political prisoners, of well-laid plans to suspend elections in 1972, of escalating provocations to justify escalating repression, of quiet preparation of NATO push-button plans so the military could take over, à la Athens. Suddenly "Z" seemed here and now, a scenario for the American present. Mayor Lindsay invited his police captains to a screening of "Z" at Gracie Mansion. They were not amused.

Not a few of America's friends wondered aloud at the possibility of crack-up, complete, total, final. Arnold Toynbee proclaimed that "to most Europeans America now looks like the most dangerous country in the world." The American danger, he said, was worse than the Russian and the heart of the danger was the Pentagon, the CIA.

"Who would have foreseen," he asked, "that America would repudiate George Washington's warning against entangling alliances? Or that America would cease to be a land of hope?"

Even Denis Brogan, almost an American by profession, raised his heavy eyebrows in worry. Where would it all end?

The critics examined with new and curious interest the American system. Not as sound or democratic as they once thought. Was not, after all, the President a kind of elected monarch? Wasn't that really what George Washington intended and had it not after two centuries turned out that way? Did he not possess unlimited power? Could he not in arbitrary fashion move events in any direction? Hadn't the system of balanced powers, the triangle of President-Congress-Court, whatever

its virtues for a small colonial farming country, gone completely
out of sync in an epoch in which the President controlled both
the levers of power and the media by which he could command
the public? Was it not futile to talk, as did Senator Fulbright
and other men in Congress, of righting the balance? After all
it was, in fact, obviously impossible to reform the system without changing the man, without changing the government itself.

This may have been the counsel of defeat but it was not an
isolated, vagrant counsel. It was a judgment shared by many
troubled individuals. Their pessimism was deep and it was real.
Not a few were turning back to the gloomiest of modern phi-
losophers, to Oswald Spengler and his Wagnerian vision of *The
Decline of the West*. What Spengler predicted had, indeed, come
true for Germany. Hitler's Reich, of which Spengler had been,
in part, prophet, in part, advocate, and finally enemy, had fulfilled his vision of apocalypse. The West as he defined it had
declined. The East had risen as Russia and China stepped
mightily onto the world stage. Thus it was not now too im-
probable to suppose that America, foster son of Spengler's
European West, would now take its place in the cavalcade of
tragedy. After all, America and its megalopian culture even more
nearly fulfilled Spengler's dismal blueprint than did Germany
and France. It did not seem unreasonable to suggest that it was
America's turn to follow Europe into Spenglerian "Caesarism"
and inevitable extinguishment in what he called the "period of
the contending states."

It is chilling but true that there is more of Spengler's
philosophy in our bloodstream than many of us realize. Spengler
insisted, again and again, that "man is a beast of prey," that man
was a barbarous, warlike creature, that hate was basic to humanity, that it was by and through killing that the superiority
of race was established.

These are strong words and strong concepts. But they bear
a suspiciously close connection to the fashionable fad for Konrad

Lorenz's *On Aggression,* for Robert Ardrey's concepts of man, the animal, of territoriality, of Desmond Morris's instinct-ridden *Naked Ape.* And, like it or not, and I do not like it at all, when we look about we do see the reality of man the murderer, the destroyer, the only creature which wars on his own, which kills for the sake of the kill not for the sake of survival, which kills and kills and kills, never more hideously than when killing his own fellow man, his own species, his own tribe, his own family, and which alone in our knowledge of nature exterminates species after species of animals, birds, reptiles, fish, plants—any protoplasm which seizes his fancy—not by some rule of survival but simply because by killing a million mosquitos he is saved from one bite, by killing a leopard he gets a dappled pattern for a woman's coat, by killing tens of thousands of mice he saves a bucket of grain.

Beautiful! I will not fault those who draw their colors for the American future from the Rothko palette, black-on-black. For we have so distorted our simple arrangements of life and existence as to place clearly and visibly before each of us the manner in which our order can be destroyed.

There are those who will impatiently say that this is an exaggeration. But there were those in Russia even after Rasputin had been poisoned, shot, stabbed, bludgeoned, and pushed through a hole in the Neva ice who blandly insisted that the Russian state and czarist society were not in danger. It was so big, so powerful. It had a great tradition, a huge army, a vast police force, an impregnable church, a mighty industrial plant, and an army of civil servants even approaching that of the United States in number and in Pecksniffianism. Business was good. Prices on the Bourse were stable. St. Petersburg's credit had gotten no worse than Washington's. The war had been going a far shorter time than Vietnam. And if, to be sure, human losses were rather higher, still it was what might be called a personnel-intensive conflict. Personnel was what Russia had plenty of;

machines and technology were in shorter supply.

I think, fortunately, that the analogy of 1916 Russia to 1970 U.S.A. is not close. Not yet. Let us not minimize, however, the fact that our system is not working well and this malfunctioning is precisely the heart of the matter. If you look at the law and the courts, which is, to be sure, the fundamental mechanism by which society manages its affairs, you will find that the American system of justice has broken down and is under savage, murderous attack—from both right and left. It is the Right against the Supreme Court. It is the Left against the whole process—courts, prosecutors, legal apparatus. It is the police against the judges whom they do not like and the controls which they abhor. It is mountebank politicians whipping up an assault on legality with law-and-order ravings. It is blue power against the dignity and humanity of the law at one end and the Chicago Seven against the Anglo-Saxon principles at the other. It is the Panthers demanding that *all* black prisoners be released from all jails. It is some police demanding the right to throw anyone *they* please into jail.

Here is the leading edge of America's special crisis. It is not, as you might suppose, the question of school desegregation (but that, too, is a matter of law, courts, justice); it is not equality of opportunity for blacks in the North (although that, in essence, is a legal question—a matter of observing laws). It is not the right of citizens to support the war or oppose it. Or even of students to obstruct the education process or plot revolution.

I will not bother to recite all the instances, but each struggle revolves around the law, around the polarization of extreme legal interpretations. The question is, Shall the Constitution prevail or shall each man, bluecoated or sweatshirted, with mace or bomb in hand, say what the law shall be? It is, thus, a question of anarchy, of whose social rules shall prevail. Or anyone's. For each extreme would destroy the Constitution. Each would destroy our system. Each would establish in its name and in its dictate a rule of terror, a rule of men unbridled and angry. And each, of course, would accomplish this "in the name of the law," "in the name of freedom," "in the name of justice." For it is a rule and has been for centuries that state crimes are always carried out in the name of the very principle which the criminal, be he prosecutor or revolutionary, is trampling to dust.

Nor should it be forgotten that great as our constitutional tradition may be, resounding as the oratory may seem, we are not, on balance, a nation where the principle of the law, of support for its letter and defense of its spirit, has unquestioned acceptance. We are a nation where vigilantism, the custom of taking "law" into popular hands, of inflicting punishment by mob action has deep, venerated roots. This was how "the West was won." This is the "justice" which is memorialized by the Western film, the cowboy classic in which good guys, as President Nixon sought to point out to his fellow lawyers, always win over the bad guys, gunning them down or hanging them with a rope thrown over the nearest tree branch without reference to judge, jury, or statute book. When trouble rises in the country the people talk more and more about the "need for action." What they mean is the need for *killing*, for killing those whom they perceive as dangers or enemies, for killing without regard for decency, for civilization, for the principles of the Constitution, or the humanitarian precepts of the Christian or Judaic faith which they pretend to observe. They speak in terms of hate. They act as Spengler said they act, "like beasts." What they speak for is murder; what they demand is blood.

If the spirit of the beast is abroad in America—what of the rest of the world?

There, surely we see no law, no order, no justice, no security —merely nations and peoples, as they have been as far back as history, tradition, and archeology can tell us, fighting and killing, wasting their substance, energy, and lives for causes which, often enough, they could not explain to the satisfaction of a child in kindergarten.

In our role as World Power, *the* World Power, as most of our statesmen and military conceive it, we have assumed a close-grained, intense, and political concern for every square mile of the earth's surface, for the totality of the sea's bottoms and the eternity of outer space. Anything, anywhere, in this world, under it or out of it, in the concepts of today's geopolitics, affects America. The concept on which foreign policy (particularly that of our military surrogates) is based out-Haushoffers Karl Haushoffer, the inventor of Nazi geopolitical theory, and makes the theses of Alexander, of Napoleon, of Ghengis Khan seem simplistic. The world conquerers of the past only sought to hold and rule what they could encompass with the force of their arms. True, they took an interest in alliances and were not indifferent to the arrangements of their enemies or possible enemies. But they did not envisage themselves as intimately concerned over the rise or fall of every political leadership in every political grouping in the world.

We do.

It is unbelievable—unbelievable but true—that our nation (regardless of its economic and military power) should deliberately, as Toynbee notes, move into such a grandiloquent posture, particularly when for fully a century of our critical early years our whole foreign policy was dominated by the wise and considered words of George Washington. If, to be sure, Washington's warning against "entangling alliances" was, in part, the wisdom of the weak, it was also wisdom won in steering a perilous course through alliances and intrigues to bring the American ship of liberty into home port, safe and free. It was a canny doctrine. William McKinley and Theodore Roosevelt shot it full of jingoist holes; Woodrow Wilson thought he could replace it with idealistic world-ism. Many have tried since to construct a sensible or grandiose concept to replace Washington's (Willkie's

One World, Clarence Streit's Union Now, the Atlantic Community, Luce's American Century). At the root of all lies the concept of American superpower, American diktat, American imposition of its code, its needs, its standards, on the world.

All of these stretch American might beyond its capability. With the rise of Soviet nuclear power, this has become clear to all but a handful of Pentagonists and their acolytes who still talk war in the terms Custer used against the Sioux: "Stop swatting flies and go for the manure heap"—as General LeMay elegantly phrases his advocacy of atombombing China.

(In such minds schemes for creating a first-strike capability which would wipe out Russia's ability to retaliate still burgeon despite the demonstrated theoretic impossibility of such a development, even if hundreds of billions more were employed in its pursuit.)

The fact is that the U.S.A. does not command the world, Harry Luce's bright words of 1941 to the contrary. The world's fate rests today on a tentative balance of nuclear terror between Moscow and Washington. Each holds back the big bang because it knows the bang is so big that Moscow can erase Washington and Washington can erase Moscow regardless of ABM's, ICBM's, MIRV's or any other acronym. We live under the peace of the drawn gun, the pistol on the table. All that can be said is that, after all, it is a peace and that the Big Two only let "small wars" (Vietnam, the Congo, Biafra, the Middle East) be fought.

But the world is in motion. The precarious balance will not hold. China is already upsetting it. Tomorrow she will be not a token nuclear-missile power but a real, if inferior, one. Technology hovers on the threshold of the Tin Lizzie A-bomb, the Henry Ford kind, turned out on a cheap production line at a cost of a few hundred thousand dollars. In other words: The dollar ante game for the big boys at the inside upstairs table at any moment (some think it has already arrived) is going to turn into penny ante. Then what—will the precarious nonproliferation agreement hold? Will Japan, India, the Arab states, Sweden, South Africa, Germany, Cuba really stand aside? Can we be sure that Israel doesn't already have a bomb or two?

We only have to read the newspapers to know how delicate the balance is where China is concerned, to watch the Russians struggle between the impulse to "take out" China's nuclear capability while there is yet time and the fear this might touch off global, final, fatal superwar.

Mene, mene, tekel. There is a global balance, of sorts, all right. But don't bet that it will last through tomorrow. If we do keep the atom bombs from exploding—what of the population bomb? There is a closer connection than many have yet noted between the danger of nuclear war and the danger that the world will drown in a sea of humanity. The equation can be clearly seen in the case of China, the world's most populous state, already teetering at the 1-billion mark. Soon after the year 2000 China will stand at the 2-billion mark. Populations are rising in Asia, Africa, Latin America, at equal rates. But the growth of food and facilities does not expand. Not that fast. Each year it drops further behind— most critically in the states whose population is exploding.

The decision which China's rulers must make (possibly before 1980) is whether to use their nuclear weapons and population superiority to procure the food and land for survival. It is this equation which understandably makes the Russians so nervous.

When we come to these questions, to nuclear warfare, to the population-food equation (and all of the implications which this equation comprehends—critical pollution of air-earth-water, exhaustion of soils, metals, natural resources, irreversible changes of the earth's temperature and climate, radical reduction of our food production capability), we come to the heart of the real crisis which faces humanity, the crisis of which the United States is only a part.

Suddenly the question broadens. It is not, Can America

survive? It is, Can humanity survive? Our primitive isolationist instinct to retreat into fortress America to fight out our purely American conflicts is exposed as being as obsolete as a Clare Briggs comic strip. Our concern over buses, taxes, hair length, sex style, rhetoric, Congress, Constitution, and even color begins to look like polymorphous perversity.

In the neurotic, bewildered, exhausted, irritable state of American society, beset with what it considers its "own" problems (the Negro with his struggle for rights and identity, the student fighting for the moral world of which he dreams, the hard hat yearning for the Fourth of July of Norman Rockwell, the policeman hoping for security, a two-car garage, and no more calls to Harlem, the politician dreaming of twenty-year seniority, a committee chairmanship, and no opposition, the military for a Culver Academy America, board chairmanships, and condominiums at Palm Springs), no one really concerns himself with Survival. We see our crisis in minimum parameter—today's in the Middle East, how to get through the next elections, keeping the dollar sound, getting the garbage off the New York streets. Those who concern themselves with tomorrow are called "visionaries," dreamers, impractical men.

Such men may be the only realists. Not many exist. There is one in Russia, Andrei Sakharov, a brilliant physicist, the scientist most responsible for the Soviet H-bomb, a genius, a man reminiscent of Einstein, of Oppenheimer, of Fermi, a man whose mind has the habit of surmounting the artificial barriers within which most of us confine our lives and which politicians erect because they are incapable of coping with anything more complex than getting through tomorrow—if that.

None of the problems with which this book deals are unfamiliar to Sakharov, although I believe he would be startled at the depth and passion stirred up by the American crisis. But the broad implications of social conflict in the twentieth century are more than apparent to him, as well as the other threats

to the existence of society. He sees them much as we do up to
a point—the dangers of nuclear war, the dangers of overpopulation, the dangers of pollution, of exhaustion of natural resources.
He sees more clearly than most Americans the unresolved dangers
centered on the emerging nationalist states, enormously fertile,
brutally deficient in technique, technology, food, and resources;
like all Russians he is acutely sensitive to the Chinese dynamic
and the threat which may flow from it.

His vision thrusts outward in other directions. He lives in
the Soviet milieu with its strict controls and restrictions (even
for a brilliant scientist like himself.) He knows the censorship,
suppression, denial of the right to criticize, to speak except with
the party voice, the barriers to travel, to interchange of ideas,
to cross-fertilization, to free and random development of the
human intellect at first hand. But his horizon is not limited to
the Soviet landscape. He comprehends the burdens which the
West imposes on the human spirit, as well as McLuhan or
Charles Reich—the soporifics of television and bulk press, the
drowning of the intellect in advertising and promotion, the in-
culcation of lumpen tastes for schmaltz and schlock, the sub-
mersion of our minds in tepid broths of mediocrity, the use of
electronic media to condition minds (including, even, the introduction of miniaturized electrodes in the brain), the employment of subliminal techniques and chemical conditioning of
attitudes.

Propagation of value standards and social motivations, based
on atavistic antimoralism, the debasement of personality by
drugs, alcohol, and other artificial means—all of these Sakharov
sees as threats to humanity and to humanity's employment of its
genius in resolving the crisis which it faces. Thus, he joins in
the Western perception of "civilized" people as being burdened
in their way by sophisticated control techniques as is Russia with
its crude and primitive reliance on the censor's shears, the control permits, the concentration camps.

Sakharov is not merely a critic of his and our society. He has a positive program for saving the world. At the center of the plan lies joint collaboration by Russia and America in the world's behalf. Only by such collaboration and by intensive, energetic, and profoundly generous use of Soviet-American resources, in his view, can the population-environmental disaster which overhangs us all be met.

But he does not rely alone on materialism. Man must be free as well as healthy. He must think as well as act. This must be true not only in the U.S.A. and the U.S.S.R. but throughout the world. To this end he proposes to put teeth into what is possibly the most optimistic statement of human intentions drafted by man in this century—the United Nations Declaration of Human Rights, a statement based on the U.S. Bill of Rights but universal. Approved more than twenty years ago, it stands today a lonely, handsome monument to man's idealism—unobserved, unenforced, unratified, largely unknown. Sakharov would make this the universal rule of the world and he would compel all nations to subordinate themselves to its word.

Of course, what Sakharov proposes is an international revolution. He would give life to the Declaration of Rights by giving the United Nations the authority and power to investigate and police violations of these rights, anywhere in the world, in big countries and in small, in Birmingham, Alabama, and in Birmingham, England, in Tashkent or Kolyma, in Brazzaville, Beirut, and Belfast, Calcutta, Canton, Capetown, or Chicago.

This would mean the yielding of national sovereignty to an international body. It would mean that the United Nations be given police forces and police powers to establish a reign of law in the world. Idealistic? Yes. As idealistic as you can get. The American and Soviet representatives bravely voted for the Declaration of Human Rights when the United Nations approved it in 1948 but neither nation has yet ratified it despite the fact that each embodies in its constitution a statement of rights and privileges very, very similar. We must conclude that neither the United States nor the Soviet Union is really interested in observing the principles for which they pretend to stand.

Why, then, advocate so radical a proposal, one which goes far deeper and cuts closer to the bone of human conduct than most of the amorphous pseudorevolutionary, cryptoanarchistic slogans of today's radical left or radical right?

Simple. Whatever the outcome of the turmoil in the United States the world's Doomsday ticks nearer. It is no longer merely the clock which the *Bulletin of Atomic Scientists* published so long on its cover to show the symbolic hour, the distance we stood from nuclear destruction (for years the clock's hands stood at five minutes to midnight). Today's Doomsday clock monitors not only nuclear confrontation. It monitors social and ecological catastrophe. While we struggle with rhetoric and bombs, trying to establish what is "relevant" for America, the world moves forward toward annihilation. It will not escape except by human effort, by the application of human resources, human intellect, human energy, human idealism. Even this may not suffice.

We will come to what must be done within our own society, within our own country, in the next chapter. Here I want to keep the emphasis on our survival in a world in which technology is creating problems far more rapidly than politics is resolving them. If we permit ourselves to turn inward from the Atlantic and Pacific, the world may simply dissolve before our eyes.

Many of use are jaded at the prospect of common cause with a Soviet Union which seems bent on emulating the more repressive and repulsive aspects of its czarist predecessor. Yet, only in partnership with Moscow can the first steps be taken toward a precarious world order; only with Moscow can we control the arms race; only with Moscow can we limit environmental contamination; only with Moscow can we hope to help less favored countries to avert the double catastrophe of famine and overpopulation; only with Russia can we begin to ease the enmities, conflicts, and passions which at any moment threaten to tear a dozen regions apart in new and savage war; only with Russia can order be brought into nuclear development to remove the threat of endless proliferation (treaty or no treaty); only with Russia can we avert the peril of turning the ocean bottom into an infinity of arms emplacements.

I am not proposing a Soviet-American world condominium. Nothing would more likely make world war certain. Nothing more likely to put the rest of the nations up against the superpowers. What I am proposing is a joint exploration, in the common interest of the U.S.A., the U.S.S.R., and the whole world, of schemes, plans, and mechanisms which will attack the most urgent international issues of the day. Nor would I for one minute limit the participation of China in such a cause. I happen to believe that China must participate as a full equal in every question of world interest. Otherwise all efforts will founder on the Chinese rock.

I have incorporated into this program some of Sakharov's ideas (like most Russians he is a China-phobe) and more of my own. It is not all embracive nor intended to be. It merely sketches the outlines of some of the things that must be done at the same time that we tackle our domestic crisis. I think it is worth pointing out that none of the programs I mention are opposed in principle by any substantial political group, party, or faction in the United States. This is not an altruistic program unless intelligent self-interest and a concern for the preservation of human life, including our own, are considered altruistic. It is founded on one simple principle: that the world has gone past the point at which it can survive new wars. I do not think we can. Nor do many people in the United States or out believe that the world can longer continue the random aggression which has marked man's rise and differentiation from other members of the animal kingdom.

Perhaps, such an approach may seem unrealistic for a nation

which is spending 70 billion dollars a year on war and arms.
I agree. That is why we must move, hand in hand, abroad and
at home. Move we must. If we imagine that we can survive
by standing where we are, by simply making limited concessions
abroad and limited corrections at home, that by passive main-
tenance of the balance of nuclear suicide we are gaining some
time—then we are sealing our own doom. In fact, we will have
signed our death warrant, that of our society and of the world.
It is too late to stand still. We must act or perish. And, in all
frankness, there is no alternative to cooperation. We can argue
about detail. Not about principle.

We can move forward abroad only, as I propose to explain
in my final chapter, if we move forward at home, not merely
to correct, to reform, to repress, to tidy up, to tinker, to wall-
paper over—but to apply the same broad philosophical principle
of cooperation, as opposed to conflict, which is the only insurance
of survival abroad.

CHAPTER 17

Will We Save It?

Thus, we round the circle. We come back to the question with which we started: Is it too late? Does doom await us, whatever we do? In fact, we have come back with an even bigger question —not just concerning our country—but the world.

The times are bad. But possibly we may hope. Perhaps, we have stronger resources than we readily perceive. In the darkest days of our Cambodian spring I was talking with a Russian friend whose judgment I respect, a Soviet social scientist who knows the United States well, who loves it and understands it, I sometimes think, rather better than we ourselves. I was surprised to find that he was not depressed by the course of American events. On the contrary he was profoundly optimistic.

"I have been coming to your country for many years," he told me. "But never have I been so impressed with your people and your spirit, with the vitality of your young people, with the courage of all Americans in struggling with the most difficult questions of the day. What other society would be so bold, so resolute, so really fine, and would labor at such great cost to find true answers to the most basic moral and political issues of the day?"

He was deeply moved. "Who could have imagined," he said, "that America, the materialistic, consumer-minded country, the country which so many of us Europeans, yes, even so many of us Russians, regards as naïve, crude, and unthoughtful, would suddenly begin to examine the central philosophical issues of mankind? It is remarkable. I can only say that I am proud of you."

Then, he added a caution which issued from the depth of his Russian experience. "You have a great country," he said. "A truly great country. Only a great country and a great people could do what you are doing. But be careful. Do not destroy it. I say that as a Russian. We Russians know the price that is paid for destruction. I do not want to see that happen in America."

I knew, of course, of what he spoke. He was evoking in those words the whole fate of Russia from 1917 to the present day—the price Russia paid in Stalinism, in terror, in repression, in lives taken or crushed, in police savagery, in paranoid repression for the liberty and idealism which possessed the first wave of revolutionaries. What he was saying was, Don't lose the liberty, the freedom, the remarkable atmosphere of America which enables you to challenge everything, to speak freely on every question, to defy your leaders, and to denounce Washington's policy. He was uttering a warning: Do not destroy what you have in trying to get something better, because what you already have is better than anything else in the world today.

This, of course, is the issue which disturbs every American except that handful dedicated to destruction, those on the left who believe that only by bringing the whole system crashing down can the new Palladium be built, those on the right who believe that only by destroying liberty can it be preserved. The lesson of those states which have attempted maximalist solutions and those revolutionaries who have contended that the worse it gets the better it gets has been a woe and grief as we saw in Hitler's Germany and Stalin's Russia. The warning must be sounded because it touches what so many of us forget.

In late summer another European Communist arrived in New York to inspect the phenomenon which so disturbs both European right and left. Would there be a revolution from the right (Europe's main fear)? Would our society simply knock itself apart? His verdict was cautiously optimistic, and despite his revolutionary philosophy he had no desire to see revolution in America. He did not think extremes were justified. To be sure, some new traumatic event could occur. Some new national tragedy, or a series of them. New lives might be taken by assassins. New atrocities might occur. Events might take a sudden unpredictable bounce. But he didn't get the smell of imminent danger. I think he is right. If we escape the destruction of our own society, there is in the flambent ingredients of American social structure today the possible components of a movement and a philosophy which could save not only ourselves but the presently doomed earth.

Much has raveled. Many have turned against the past, hate the present, fear the future. But a time of true crisis is a forge into which is tumbled the scrap iron of history, the fresh ore of the present, and the catalyst of our spirit. From this issues the bright new steel of the future.

Not many today recall what Dickens wrote in *A Tale of Two Cities* after his famous opening words, "It was the best of times and the worst of times. . . ." He went on:

"It was the age of Wisdom, it was the age of Foolishness, it was the Epoch of Belief, it was the epoch of incredulity, it was the Season of Light, it was the Season of Darkness, it was the spring of Hope, it was the winter of Despair—we had everything before us, we had nothing before us, we were all going direct to Heaven, we were all going direct the other way. In short, the period was so far like the present period that some of its noisiest authorities insisted on it being received for Good or for Evil, in the Superlative Degree of Comparison only."

Dickens was writing of the days of the French Revolution. Then, truly, to the good burghers of England the world had gone out of joint. The scent of danger was borne to English nostrils by every fog that rolled over the chalk cliffs of Dover. Who knew but that London's turn at the tumbrils and the guillotine was next!

The world was tumbling down. The very bricks seemed to be flying from the chimneys. Where was the man to cry courage to the doomed, confidence to the despairing, vision to the bewildered?

There was, of course, no answer in logic and reason. Nor should one be sought today. Man's greatest, most touching delusion is that of his rationality, his ability to analyze with accuracy and act with precision and clarity. Stalin boasted of his "steel logic." It seemed like steel to his pitiable subjects. But it was founded on paranoia. Find a "logical" statesman, a "logical" leader, and you have found a prescription for disaster. There was no logic in Churchill's bravado after Dunkirk but it saved England.

Robert McNamara's computers did not lie when they told him the application of X power would produce Y victories in Southeast Asia. But they were not programmed for human beings. They were programmed for electronic guidance systems.

People are not steel and concrete and semiconductors and multiple independently targeted rockets carrying megaton warheads of fusionable hydrogen. They are not subliminal subjects to be cozened and manipulated, their emotions played by the programmer at the console of a titanic supercomputer. Why have we made myth of Moses in the wilderness? Washington at Valley Forge? Because of the vigor and clarity of their logic? No. Because their mad unreason was greater than reason, stronger than logic.

Man is irrational, impulsive, stubborn, interreactive, warm, vengeful, delusional, illusional, humanitarian, genocidal, tribal, racial, loving, principled, cunning, comradely, his own worst enemy, the worst enemy of every form of life, the greatest danger to himself and to the world. The prime destroyer! But he is also the builder, the creator, the savior, if savior exists. He is the transmitter of the world's heritage, insofar as it is preserved; only he can save himself.

This sounds like a sermon. It must be. Because in the real and primitive sense (long since forgotten amid ritual and sodden systematization) the sermon is the word by which man keeps alive the torch which he lighted and which only he can keep alive.

You may say that the fire *can* go out. True. It can. But it never has. You may say that humanity can be extinguished, that our way of life, the structure of our society, can be wiped out or transformed. True. It can.

Underlying these words there is a kind of cataclysmic psychology. We feel that the issues of the day are so profound that we may not survive their resolution. But the resilience of human systems is inevitably greater than is perceived in the moment of despair.

We can survive. If we believe we can. We can do more. We can build upon these extraordinary times. We can rally the magnificent energy, the flaming idealism, the powerful energies of all of our peoples—the young with their new life-styles, the old with their retrospective vision, the blacks with their dynamism and dignity, the frustrated middle class, the upward-mobile proletariat, which can be the most powerful estate of all.

This we can accomplish if we know what we are about. What do we really want for America? Are we really so far apart? Is there one among us who does not want justice and equity for himself? Is there one who would deny it to his fellow citizens?

I think not. I think neither radical nor conservative opposes justice for all. Do we wish to tear our nation and its institutions apart with punitive assaults and deadly explosives? I think not. I do not believe blacks like to live by the rifle. I am certain the police do not deliberately walk with drawn pistols. The Nechaevs of today did not come willingly to nitroglycerine and clock fuses. Is there any issue which so divides America that it cannot be talked through to resolution? I think not. President Johnson liked to say in those endless bouts of verbal exercise to which he was pathologically addicted, "Come, let us reason together." It is time we heed his advice. Our nation was built on passion, on argument, on conflict. It can only grow stronger by renewing the old tradition.

There are those who say that no plan will work, that all counsel will fail unless the atmosphere is changed. I am inclined to agree. What is needed is a new climate. This is the most difficult act, particularly with a national leadership founded on the principle of small steps, of balanced deeds, of moving cautiously, or not at all.

But I submit there is one act which will galvanize our spirit. Stop the war in Vietnam.

Oh, yes. I know how often this has been said before. Yes, I know how much we want to hear something magic, something new, something that comes on like Joe Namath. The days of magic, alas, are over. But Vietnam goes on draining its poison into our systems, tainting one generation after another, spreading over the land like deadly smog.

But we must begin, I think, with the war—for moral reasons, for practical reasons of economics, and, perhaps most of all, for the release of energy and human spirit which its end will bring.

Let us put morals first because it is the moral question which underlies most of the issues which concern America. To young Americans (and many others) Vietnam is simply the question of callous taking of human life against every precept for which our society is said to stand. This government-directed, government-sponsored killing, this harnessing of our scientific-technological-economic apparatus to the mass taking of human life seems to many to render hypocritical every effort to defend the principles of our society. It is, many feel, merely a huge death-producing machinery in which the state and industry have joined hands.

This argument is so powerful that it has undercut the confidence of even those who struggle most patriotically to support the war. They, too, feel something is wrong, although perhaps not being certain just what it is.

If we end the war we take the first step, both at home and abroad, toward erecting a new and better system, a system of no-war and of cooperation abroad, a release of our technical and economic resources into life-preserving, life-enhancing, life-improving purposes at home, and an end to the deepest schism in our moral structure.

But this is only a start.

If you look at the slogans of dissent you will find that they are almost universally negative. The young say, Stop the War. Halt the spending on arms. Stop the killing. The blacks say, End discrimination. End coercion. End the killing of blacks. The Middle Americans say, End the disorder. End the threat to our homes, our security, our way of life.

All negatives and each, filled with moral fervor, filled with a fiery sense of injustice, an intolerance for further evil, sees solutions written only in anger and blood. The system, each says, has ceased to work, or works only against him.

These negatives are typical, I must note, of revolutionary moods. In 1776 it was, George III must go! In France it was, To the guillotine! In Russia it was, Down with the Czar!

Our own mood may not yet approach such simplistic slogans but there is diminishing confidence that our institutions can be made to serve the purposes for which they were created; the courts seem to be breaking down; the prisons have taken on a medieval aspect; justice does not work; Congress is not responsive; the President is too powerful or not powerful enough; elections are farces; business is repressed or is perceived as inhumane; blacks see themselves confronted with the ultimate violence of the state; whites fear black reprisals; the old fear the young; the young the old.

So the melancholy circle goes. There is no panacea, nor do revolutionaries or reactionaries profess to have one. Each hopes to use and advocates the use of force against the other. None possesses a positive program other than imposition of his special morality upon those he sees as enemies.

The circle can be broken only by dynamic charisma. I mean, quite simply, a leader, a man willing to say the obvious; that he is prepared to cut our war budget to $20 billion a year, the first year, and put $50 billion to work for schools, jobs, health, environment, housing, and the other social ills which cover America like gray sludge. For the first year, that is. The next year, after making a basic agreement with the Soviet for a defensive standstill and cooperation, he offers $20 billion to the world to begin the task of easing social-economic-health-pollution problems in Asia, Africa, and Latin America. He goes on from there.

Oh, I know everyone will argue over such a program. Will this end the bombing of university buildings, the slaughter of blacks, the poisoning of our cities and waterways, the depredation of our environment by profit-hungry industry?

No. Let's face it. It does not cure all our ills. Did Washington end America's problems when he won the war against England? Did Lincoln solve the Negro problem by defeating the Confederacy? Did Lenin cure Russia's backwardness by seizing power on November 7, 1917?

Of course not. You cannot cure society overnight. With a

revolution or without. With a program or without. Most revolutionary programs rear back on their creators and cause ills at least
as great as those they are supposed to cure. Roosevelt's New Deal
has left our society a heritage of festering problems—for example,
slum clearance which gives us skyscraper ghettos worse than the
old-law tenements.

Don't expect to change it all whether you burn it down or
impose "law and order" at the point of a tommygun. It can't be
done. All you can do, really, is to make people *feel* better. But we
can do one big thing. We can tackle head-on the sphere into which
human beings put more time, money, and technique than any
other: War.

End that threat. Bring it under control. Taper down the arms
race. Halt the nuclear insanity. Make space exploration collabora-
tive. Do that and we will have the money, the personnel, the
energy, the spirit, the moral strength to cope with the other grave
ills of our society and the world: population pressure, environmental debasement, food shortages, illness, ignorance, human
hostility.

I know that many think only a neat tabulated political program is the answer. Let me ask this: Where does such a program
exist and when did *any* national leader ever carry one out? National leaders come into office with negative programs. They are
against many evils and especially the evil of their opponent. Then
they spend their lives improvising positive programs and if they
are realists, pragmatists, they change and change and change
again because neither they nor we are perfect. Perfectionism is
simply a symptom of profound neurosis.

I can hear the young chanting, Cop-out! Only revolution
will change the old order and clear the site for building the new
Utopia. Maybe. I agree with Sakharov's wry calculation that we
can't afford a revolution. The cost of the destruction, the loss of
production, the loss of the normal gain in GNP takes from society,

especially the lowest, most economically deprived elements, far more than could be gained if the factories go on, if the assembly lines continue to function. The poor lose the most from revolution, particularly in affluent, highly productive societies like the U.S.A.

Change—yes. Destruction—no.

I can hear the tired middle-aged query: Will it work? Will they cut their hair and stop the bombing?

Does anyone *really* think that long hair has anything to do with politics? Was it long hair that made George Washington lead a revolution? Did Abraham Lincoln's chin whiskers give him moral stature?

Bombs. That is another question. The bombs are evidence of the terrible fissures in our society. The fissures will widen, the structure will crack unless we act *positively* to build a better society. I think that if we end the war and use the enormous resources of the arms race for positive not negative purposes, we can bring life to the ethics and morals and ideas we think we believe in.

The blacks will say, What about Watts? What about Harlem? What about the South Side? What about Mississippi? We don't buy it.

I say OK. Let's be fair. Let's put the bulk of that $50 billion that we divert from war and arms into help for the bottom people, black and marginal whites. Let's concentrate our programs at the low end of the scale. With that impetus it should not take long to produce a radical shift in the income pattern of our society—to wipe out the bottom of the spectrum, to end poverty in America, to attain the age-old dream of man by eliminating need and want.

Civil Rights: Put the U.N. Declaration of Rights to work.

The Hard Hats. Will they say, No! I think not. Are they or anyone against better pay, better living standards, security, a square deal, an end of world conflict and tensions, an end to losing sons in far-off Asian lands? Of course not. The Hard Hat is too big and tough to admit it. But what sends his adrenalin up is fear—fear that someone else is going to take his job, fear that someone else may change his life, fear of the unknown, the uncertain, the new and the different.

Of course, I can hear the older generation harrumph: That's a lot of fine talk. Suppose you do stop the war—how do you get all this going?

I say, let's go back to beginnings. Washington and Jefferson and Hamilton and the rest invented a good product. We are the ones who debased it. Let's give it a new shine. I can't tell you how much I distrust the futurists who make up brand-new game plans, laboratory visions, or new constitutions, new ways of organizing society. I believe in change, even radical change, but only after peering deeply into the past in order to understand the present more clearly.

I believe that the past gives us insight into the future and enables us to spin the wheels of history in the direction we want to go. I believe in harnessing the forces of change to those of continuity. I do not believe we must burn the building down to destroy the rats, nor that we must turn the building into an Orwellian asylum to protect it from destruction. The only purpose of the building, that is to say, our constitutional system, is to create the best possible environment for us, the people. It is not designed to provide for infinitely expanding law practice, infinitely expanding corporate profits, infinitely expanding government bureaucracy, infinitely expanding idiosyncratic life-styles. It is, like all such documents, imperfect. But burning will not improve it. Nor will writing out a new set of rules on neat pieces of paper. The only thing that will make society run better and the Constitution work better is better people working more honestly to make it work better.

If that sounds old-fashioned—so be it. I am, as I have said, old-fashioned in my views of my country. The old American dream may not be the last best bright hope of humanity. But find me a better one. The problem is not the dream; it is its realization.